Unbiased Investor

Unbiased
Investor

Reduce Financial Stress and Keep More of Your Money

Coreen Sol

WILEY

For general information on our other products and services or for technical support, please
contact our Customer Care Department within the United States at (800) 762-2974,
outside the United States at (317) 572-3993 or fax (317) 572-4002.

Wiley also publishes its books in a variety of electronic formats. Some content that appears
in print may not be available in electronic formats. For more information about Wiley
products, visit our web site at www.wiley.com.

Library of Congress Cataloging-in-Publication Data is Available:

ISBN 9781394150083 (Hardback)
ISBN 9781394150106 (ePDF)
ISBN 9781394150090 (epub)

Cover Design: Wiley
Cover Image: © phipatbig/Shutterstock

SKY10036141_092322

For biased people everywhere, because without the intervention of behaviour, returns would be little more than the inflation rate.

And especially for Jakob, Eiden and Sofia, OFC, my greatest joys.

Contents

Introduction
The Path of Least Resistance

D o you tend to act more like water or electricity?

Imagine a single electrical current that feeds two lights. The first light is a 60-watt classic incandescent bulb. The other is a modern 8.5-watt low-resistance LED (light-emitting diode). When a wire conducts current to both circuits at the same time, surprisingly, both lights brighten up! That is to say, electricity has no preference for the lower-resistance LED bulb.

In contrast, water always takes the path of least resistance. It never runs uphill, and if there's an easier route, water will find it.

In our lives, the path of least resistance is the easiest road to travel, but it's a choice, nevertheless. We are more than capable of solving both simple and complicated problems – to venture down both low- and high-resistance paths. But it's naturally appealing to use the least amount of effort.

Most people understand the effects of procrastination on their ability to complete tasks and reach personal goals. For example, say that you commit to a morning exercise regime before work. As the alarm jumps

1

to life at 6 a.m., it's easy to convince yourself to stay under the blankets instead of leaping out of bed into your shorts and runners. Procrastination is the preference for immediate payoffs over future rewards – the cozy bed versus a fit body. Despite your best intentions, this bias begs you to take the path of least resistance.

Beyond the persuasion that bias play over your fitness and other personal goals, it can also prompt you to save and spend money in certain predictable ways that we have come to understand over recent years. While the sway of bias is often subtle, it can produce damaging outcomes when it incites anxiety in your financial decisions or results in judgment errors and even financial loss. And, despite the potentially harmful impact on your financial well-being, most people are unaware of the vast majority of these naturally occurring tendencies, when these behaviors occur, and how to intervene.

Over the last three decades, I've been involved in behavioral finance research, both formally, as an adjunct professor at the University of British Columbia Okanagan, and practically, as a CFA charterholder and discretionary portfolio manager. It has been fascinating to observe the wide variety of ways clients formulate decisions during the emotional ups and downs of significant events such as the Asian, Russian, and Argentine economic crises of the 1990s; the September 11, 2001, terrorist attacks; countless energy calamities; acute weather events; the Great Recession of 2008, and the 2020 worldwide pandemic. Despite the variety of circumstances, I have found that most investors are relatively consistent in their behavioral approach, following similar patterns when events recur. As markets drop precipitously, it became predictable which clients would call, who I'd need to reassure, and which people would be motivated to change their investment policies whenever volatility escalates.

It was also telling that when certain clients called the office with fear about the prevailing havoc in the investment markets, the timing of those calls was almost always at or near the trough of the market cycle. It was these experiences that inspired me to learn about the influences over people's ability to make prudent financial decisions. The lessons and strategies I've learned over the last 30 years of managing people and their wealth are in this book.

Errors of judgment are not restricted to the urge to sell your investments at the bottom of a stock market decline. They crop up in your daily routines when you least expect them. They affect how much you spend, how much you save, and how you negotiate contracts. The instances that erode your wealth go largely undetected, with each of us commonly justifying these occurrences by attributing them to some other set of facts.

Consider how frenzied trading activity recently inspired by Reddit and other social media platforms pushed up the stock price of Game-Stop by a hundredfold over a few weeks. The business prospects of the company were no better after its price skyrocketed than before the increase. Something else must be at work – something in the behavior of the masses who participated, all believing that buying the shares was a good idea at that time.

This isn't the only example of investors willing to convince themselves that trading overpriced investments somehow makes sense. The justifications that we manufacture only serve to make us feel better about our moment-driven choices. The security is overpriced, yet we decide to buy it anyway. Then, we follow-up the transaction with another natural inclination, which is to confirm our decision. If the price appreciates after we make the investment, we believe this to be evidence of a wise choice. The rising price of an overpriced-stock, however, doesn't change the fact that it is overvalued. And, despite the enthusiasm of those investors participating in the short-run gains, the risks of repricing at the lower reasonable value intensify the higher it goes.

We similarly excuse poor decisions on some external factor when investment values drop. There is always a handy justification at the ready. Either way, we want to feel that we made the right decision, whether it was a prudent investment or not.

Many examples of judgment errors don't seem like errors at all. Take, for example, investors who refuse to hold a certain a type of security because they lost money on such a trade in the past. Surely, it's a good idea to avoid earlier mistakes, isn't it? Yet relying categorically on this rule of thumb has limited these investors from participating in opportunities that may be suitable, profitable in the future, or otherwise provide important advantages.

Behavioral bias doesn't only affect individual investments, but can also cause general patterns across the capital markets as a whole. Investors' decisions – inspired by common biases – can result in broad market

changes. Stock market prices can regularly become overheated in a tide
of euphoria, or be demolished by sweeping fear. Collectively executed
behavior manifests in overbought and oversold stocks until enough
individuals realize the error and abandon the buying or selling frenzy.
Prices rise or fall much further than is warranted by fundamentals when
bias distorts our analysis and overrules our long-term strategies.

Academics have debated whether markets are efficient since stock
analysis became a recognized profession. There is educated rationale
argued on both sides. However, profitable investing boils down to one
truth. If investors know all the reported information about a company and
information is widely distributed, there should be little to dispute the value
of any stock or other investment. If the company's shares trade below
that value, a shrewd investor will buy them, pushing the share price up
to that value until no further profit can be made. If the shares trade above
this value, they sell it (or short it), pushing the price down to this value. If
we all agree on the value of anything – through analysis – there would be
little or no profit able to be made on trading it, beyond the internal growth
of the business. But, in real life, it is much more complicated because
people – endowed with prejudices and judgment errors—are part of the
decision process. So, it is these distortions that provide another way to
profit: when other investors are wrong and you recognize the mistake.

As we continue to increase our understanding of behavioral economics, investors can use that information to produce better decisions,
reduce the stress in financial transactions, and increase long-term financial gains. As you discover the impact of certain conditions on your
behavior, you'll become empowered to modify your choices and
increase your opportunities to succeed.

This book is designed to help you identify how and when bias
undermines your financial decisions and how to mitigate the damage it
can cause. By determining your personal set of values and by building a
long-term perspective of your goals, you can limit the number of financial decisions you will face over your life, and in turn, lessen the effects
of potential mistakes.

This book also provides you with simple habits that you can incorporate into your lifestyle to avoid many of the pitfalls that you'll learn
about. With these strategies, you can reduce your risk and limit the
worry of economic losses.

Behavioral economics is a relatively new field, yet the vast body of work has resulted in a dictionary-long list of behavioral terms. Many of these definitions are overlapping or interconnected, if not confusing. Moreover, many of the biases identified by research are tough to avoid in a meaningful or pragmatic way. To counteract this impracticality, I developed an overarching structure that puts the large number of recognized biases into three categories so that investors can more easily identify the underlying processes that effect their decisions.

Most biases fit into one of three primary processes:

1. We rely on rules of thumb and other efficiency mechanisms to understand our world, which can distort our judgment.
2. We try to control the risks we face, sometimes at the worst possible moment.
3. We have a strong predisposition to believe that we are right, even if this belief is misguided.

A single defined-bias is rarely the sole influence of our choice architecture. Our actions typically manifest from a variety of interacting biases at once. For example, the tendency to hold onto losing stocks and sell the winning ones is described by the **disposition effect, loss aversion,** and **anchoring**. The willingness to buy inflated stocks is tied to **overconfidence, confirmation bias,** and **herd mentality**. Each of these biases – and others – will be discussed in the pages to follow, organized by these categories in Chapters 1 to 3: Making Sense of What You See; Controlling Risk; and Wanting to Be Right.

Understanding when biases are present is important because they can seem deceptively logical. You may feel that you have determined your best option; however, the fundamental way that your brain manages data, with shortcuts and time-saving strategies, causes systematic problems that you may not yet recognize.

It is critical to first be able to identify which situations commonly interfere with your financial success. To that end, the first chapter describes a variety of scenarios where bias can cause distortions and judgment anomalies. The second chapter outlines how your attempts to control risk can undermine your goals and objectives. The third chapter illustrates a variety of ways that our deep-seated desire to substantiate our decisions – prove that we are correct – can alter our perceptions. In the stories ahead, you will likely relate to many of the examples because behavioral biases are startlingly consistent among all of us. You may recognize situations that you've been in, both past and present, and you may identify with the various decision-making processes and justifications. In any event, you'll notice how simple, yet dastardly, these inclinations can be in undermining your financial success. The innocuous nature of these tendencies may even induce you to feel that you can avoid such errors in the future, now that you're aware of them. That's natural, and if you find yourself feeling that way, you'd be falling under the spell of another bias! Knowing is not enough, as you'll discover during the investigation of the **G.I. Joe Fallacy**.

Nevertheless, you can correct for many of these predispositions with the relatively simple habits that this book offers. If you've ever relied on an alarm clock, you've already applied a conventional technique to control your behavior. Incorporating other habits in your lifestyle can similarly improve your financial success.

In addition to distilling the list of individual biases into the three primary patterns of errors, this work serves up a single critical strategy to apply to all aspects of your financial affairs. By honing your choices to align with your values and long-term plans instead of making reactionary choices, you can reduce the number of overall decisions that you need to execute. This will reduce your exposure to behavioral biases and reduce the stress of confronting such decisions, by reducing their frequency.

When you understand your motivations and your objectives, you can avoid considerable heartache over your lifetime. The only way to consistently integrate your values into your financial decisions is to know what they are first. Many people have a loose idea of what they value, but few people take the necessary steps to organize them into a practical and usable process. By following the eight steps in Chapter 4, you can uncover your financial motivations and identify what is most important to you. Ultimately, the responses to each activity are driven by you and will likely be very different from your neighbor. That is what makes them powerful in your pursuits and in maintaining your distinct financial objectives. These questions were developed from my experience working with a wide variety of individuals of all levels of wealth and used in my investment practice today.

At the end of the eight activities, you will have a tool that can help you achieve your most critical goals. Applying your **personal economic values (PEVs)** to long-view decisions will limit the impact of herd mentality, loss aversion, and a host of other traps. The fewer times you change your mind, the fewer decisions you'll make, and the less you'll be subject to errors in judgment.

By engaging your PEVs, you will be empowered to reduce the stress of financial decisions because you can avoid transactional decisions and remain focused on what is most critical to you. Chapters 5 and 6 look at the strategies that I have been helping my clients to implement for decades.

Calculated consistent choices aligned with your values will help you to behave like electricity, choosing your route, rather than flowing like water down the path of least resistance. Ultimately, you are pursuing your personal version of happiness. As the age-old question begs: Can money buy happiness? Follow-up questions are, then, if it can, how does it work? How much of it do you need? And how do you attain it? Chapter 7 offers insights into what you may have felt for years, backs it up with research, and distills it into effective habits that you can adopt in your life.

The objective of this book is to reduce your stress in financial decisions, produce more reliable outcomes, and limit your financial risks. While this book offers a generous helping of the knowledge that I have accumulated from working with a wide variety of clients, the information contained in these pages is not investment advice nor can it take your particular circumstances into account. If, by the end of this book, you find any product or service discussed appealing, I urge you to seek an investment professional who can explore whether such approaches are right for you. Also, I'd like to point out that the views set out in this book are well-researched from sources that I believe to be credible and reliable. I'd also like to assert that professional organizations that I work with now or have worked with in the past represent a wide body of individuals and opinions, and the conclusions of my work may not be held by these respected organizations.

Chapter 1

Making Sense
of What You See

ANCHORING: An Invisible Hand

when your investments
peak at a high watermark
you can't forget it

Suppose that you are in the market for a new car and your heart's set on an electric vehicle. The lower operating costs or the reduced environmental impact has you scouring the internet for various options when you settle for a Nissan Leaf. Various websites indicate that the manufacturer's suggested retail price (MSRP) is approximately $45,000 in 2021. That number is your starting point. It's your anchor, or more precisely, it's the anchor that Nissan has planted in your mind. You'll never agree to pay more than that price unless there are extra features (a separate value), and you likely believe that you'll negotiate a lower price at the showroom.

If you hadn't known the price beforehand and thought the car would cost $30,000, that would have been your initial anchor and you'd likely be turned off to discover that it was $15,000 more. Conversely, if your impression was that it would run near $60,000, you'll be pleased to discover that you won't be shelling out as much as you thought. Disappointment is unavoidable when the retail price is higher than your expectation. However, a lower price elicits the opposite, positive emotional kick. You might even feel as though you've saved some money.

The difference between your perception and reality induces feelings about the transaction. Since the purchase price is the same in both cases, your reaction results from your initial ideas, not from the price itself. Not only do you feel good or bad based on your earlier expectations, but the difference may also inspire or deter you from actually buying the car. You are not emotionally tied to the item's price as much as you are tied to the difference between what you thought it was and the actual cost.

Like most people, you prefer to believe that your choice is free from outside influences. It is reassuring to think that you use independent thought processes to determine the price to pay for the new car – or anything else, for that matter. After all, you rely on evidence and logic to reach decisions. Even when you don't know all the facts, you can form a reasonable guess founded on other facts that you know.

However, **anchoring** has an unyielding influence over your financial decisions because your starting point influences not only your emotional response but also your negotiations, the final price that you pay, and even whether you will proceed with the transaction. Anchors are insidious and especially corrupt when the anchor originates from an external source or is completely unrelated.

You're probably already aware of the enticing nature of a sale price. A discounted price can even motivate you to purchase something you hadn't intended to buy. When you see a tag with an original price tag listing a lower sale price below it, chances are that you will not be able to forget the original price, even if you believe you have. Retailers know this, which is why they don't list the sale price in isolation. The regular price is always listed next to the temporary discount. Since retail and sale prices are largely arbitrary, it's an affront to post one beside the other to affect how we feel about buying an item.

Despite what you may believe about your ability to discard your earlier ideas and conclusions, you likely won't be able to let go of an anchor completely. Even when the initial anchor is grossly too high or too low, you'll be tempted to believe that you have disassociated from it because it is obviously incorrect or irrelevant. That process is misleading because instead, it remains in the back of your mind as a starting point to adjust from, and it will ultimately influence you.

An early study on the effects of anchors had participants spin a wheel rigged to randomly land on either 10 or 65. They were each asked if the number of African countries in the United Nations was higher or lower than the result that they spun on the wheel.[1]

Without an exact answer, most people run through a process to recall some nugget of relevant information from their bank of experiences. You may visualize the massive continent on a map nestled between the Atlantic and Indian Oceans. Perhaps a wildlife program about the exotic indigenous animals in the region, or maybe a recent conversation about the cultural experience shared by a friend who traveled to Africa, comes to mind. In any event, you realize the vast size of the area. You rely on whatever resources you have at your disposal to form an estimation.

Imagine that you are participating in the experiment and spin the number 65. You may realize that 65 is too large a number to be accurate, quickly concluding that the number of African countries in the United Nations is some lesser quantity. Conversely, you'd draw the opposite conclusion if you land on 10. The experiment then proceeds to ask participants to estimate the actual number.

The results were compelling. Those who spun the result of 65 estimated 45 African countries, while those who landed on 10 estimated a mere 25 countries. The random numbers on a wheel obviously have nothing to do with Africa or the United Nations, yet the anchor significantly impelled the participants' answers.

These results are not limited to experimental studies. This is common across everyday decisions, yet individuals are often unaware of the connection between anchors and conclusions. Moreover, these effects seem particularly underhanded when the anchor is entirely unrelated to the question at hand.

Imagine that you're asked to provide the last two digits of your phone number, and then to estimate your expected returns over the next 10 years. You may think, "Well, my phone number has nothing to do with my investments," and you honestly believe you have discarded these unrelated numbers as you estimate your returns. However, it is more likely that you'll follow the same process as the participants in the United Nations study. Once you acknowledge that your phone number is irrelevant, you then pick a number that is higher or lower than the two digits that you recalled. Regardless of whether you believe that you have discarded the unrelated numbers, you will likely be tied to them insofar as they are your starting point (anchor) and you then proceed to make some adjust from it to resemble what your expected returns are.

From countless studies and experiments using anchors, the issue with this process is that people tend to be too conservative in how far they adjust from the anchor. In this case, if your phone number ends in 87, your expected returns will be far higher than if it ends in 02. Your expected return will be within the realm of possibilities, but your anchor will influence your final estimation.

Consider when, instead, your anchor is the returns you achieved last year, and your results were unusually high. While you adjust your expectations lower for the following year, you will still likely overshoot realistic expectations. Then you may find yourself disappointed when these high returns don't pan out, especially since you went through the process of reducing your hopes. Likewise, if investment yields were low last year, so too will be your expectations for the next.

In any event, actual investment returns will most likely be closer to normal long-run averages than abnormally high or low for the following year, so basing next year's returns on last year's in any way is not particularly insightful, given the influence that anchoring plays in the result. It would be better to recalibrate and assume that your returns will be whatever the long-term average is for your type of investment, without making any adjustments.

An anchor is nearly impossible to abandon, even for professionals who pride themselves on impartial evaluation. In one such test, real estate agents were asked to assess the price of a home listed for sale. The agents visited the property and reviewed a wide range of information on the house, including the listing price. Half of the realtors were given a substantially higher listing price than the others, and each realtor was then asked to provide a reasonable price for the property. They were also requested to determine the lowest price at which they would agree to sell the house if they owned it.

When the agents were asked how they formed their opinion, they claimed that the house list price was not a factor. Many of them also claimed to take pride in ignoring the list price as irrelevant in their independent analysis. Despite the agents' insistence that the initial anchor price was not part of their determination, those who were given the higher listing price estimated the sale price to be 41% more.[2]

Anchoring is embedded in all monetary decisions because invariably, there are numbers in every financial choice. The inability to completely detach from an anchor (or sufficiently adjust from it) is a problem for investors. In another common example, consider an investor who buys a stock solely because the price has dropped. Stocks aren't like a pair of shoes with a consistent value that you can buy on sale – the value of a business changes due to changing economics and prospective earnings.

It is also common to justify that a share price will bounce back to the last higher price after a drop, even if there are economic reasons for the new price. It is a conventional error to assume that the stock market price is always the proxy for the value of the company's shares because sometimes securities are mispriced – often due to investors' biases. A stock price doesn't always reflect the company's value or economic outlook. More importantly, its historical share price does not predict the company's future. Nevertheless, people mistakenly rely on previous price patterns to indicate future performance.

Consider Vermilion Energy Inc. (VET). During the summer of 2014, the share price topped $77.92, at a time when a barrel of West Texas Oil was worth over US$100 (Source: Refinitiv). Following a massive deterioration in oil prices in the following year, oil companies around the world suffered significant share price declines. To this day, investors – especially those who were intimately involved in the oil heydays of the 1990s – freely comment that oil companies are cheap. When you believe that a share price is undervalued, you'll naturally conclude that the price should rise. But, the current market price of a security should already reflect all known information about the industry and economic prospects of the company. If it was undervalued, someone would buy it to profit, thereby pushing the price of the shares up. If you decided that it was a bargain to buy VET shares at half their earlier market value, you'd be disappointed that, six years later, VET continued to languish in the single digits (Source: Refinitiv). It is only once the price of oil increases when the prospects of the business rises and the share price will follow, not because it was that price in the past.

Believing that the earlier price of a stock infers some information about its prospects is baseless. Think of this another way: ABC shares are trading at $40. Your sister bought shares of ABC at $28. Your friend bought them at $38, and you purchased the shares at $43. Whose purchase price reflects the value of the stock? You can't answer the question based on the share price alone, yet anchoring leads us to falsely believe that it holds useful information.

Also, if enough investors see patterns in price changes and act on them, the pattern itself can become a self-fulfilling prophesy. So-called technical analysts attempt to predict future price movements based on past prices and volumes. This technique may actually be rooted in identifying behavioral motivations of mass groups of investors. If stock prices reflect investors' collective decisions, and people are generally biased in comparable ways, technical analysis may be onto something. But if that's true, then it will be rendered ineffective if people control for bias.

Similar to the belief that a stock can return to an earlier higher price, the **anchoring bias** coaxes investors to cling to the high-water mark of an entire investment portfolio. Once the value of your investment account has touched peak value, it's almost impossible to forget it. When the market value of your savings reaches $10,000, or $100,000 or $10,000,000 before retreating (due to normal market fluctuations), you'll always reflect on the fact that it was that value at one time. You will likely also feel a sense of loss if the value is currently lower than that high-water mark, even if you've earned excellent profits on your portfolio at the value that it stands.

You'll also be more likely to hold onto your investments if they are lower than the high-water mark, feeling tempted to wait out the return to the higher value. This assumes that the portfolio value will rise again to former highs regardless of what available economic evidence may suggest.

Anchoring distorts your perception of performance and the value of an investment. It can influence you to hold an asset too long and may lead you to buy investments – or other goods – for no other reason than the current price relative to the anchor. Regardless of the situation, where anchors are present, they can affect your decisions in predictable ways, even when the anchoring number is unrelated. Unfortunately, unless you know about the problems anchoring causes, the effect goes largely undetected. Generally, people are unaware that an anchor is so deceptive or that their decisions are less independent than they believe.

It is important to note that investments reflect expected future returns (or income) and account for variances in the economic outlook. Neither a security's price nor a portfolio's past value can be a crystal ball for its future performance. That is why regulators caution investors with the disclaimer, "Past performance is not an indication of future returns."

REPRESENTATIVENESS: If It Walks Like a Duck

reading book titles
helps to pick a good story
except when it doesn't

Imagine that you're sitting in a taxi in downtown Edinburgh when it strikes you that the people of Scotland are much more lighthearted than people back home in Toronto. You recall the couple you met on the street who stopped to provide directions and a lighthearted quip about the city. "In Scotland, there's no such thing as bad weather, only the wrong coat."

Your mind wanders back to when you first arrived in the country a couple of days ago, and each instance of a cheerful exchange since you landed. Some of the people were downright funny, cracking jokes even though you were a complete stranger. In stark contrast, no one would dare to share a "good morning" during your brisk walk along Yonge Street.

Upon your return, you repeatedly describe the Scottish people as unusually friendly and even comical, drawing on a few experiences to describe an entire nation. Of course, you mean to apply the characterization loosely and expect your audience to understand that not all Scottish people are natural comedians! Still, a grain of truth resonates. You honestly believe that there is more humor in Scotland than Canada.

Representativeness helps us to sort information into categories and draw conclusions more efficiently. For example, it is common to rely on a small sample of data, or some other proxy, to represent the larger whole. We often take the narrow selection and apply it to the entire group.

Drawing on limited information to make decisions is a reasonable approach when you don't have anything else to work with. If you only have a few details, it's the only practical way to form an opinion. Nevertheless, you likely understand that drawing broad sweeping conclusions from minimal amounts of data is perilous. A small sample rarely represents a large body accurately, yet sorting, counting, and summarizing your experiences into these limited representations are a convenient way to make sense of the world. Sometimes, however, this processing shortcut results in misinterpreting how closely related two things or events may be. We often jump to a comparison too quickly and make assumptions about how similar the representation is of the whole group when it may not be as closely related as is seems at first glance.

As obviously biased as this approach is, it's typically taken for granted. And just as ironically, people tend not to apply this process in reverse! We tend to disregard broad truths when it comes to a specific case. We're inclined to excuse individual instances as an exception to the rule, and consider each situation to be unique or unrelated to average results. This is especially true when the circumstance involves us directly. If each instance is uncommon, however, then that shared distinction makes them similar, or even average. Each of us is unique, just like everyone else!

Think about when someone is rude or cuts you off in traffic. It's easy to conclude that they are an unpleasant person or a terrible driver. Yet, when you act the same way, you will be tempted to attribute the behavior to an exclusion. We are not poor drivers or rude, instead we pass off our lapse in judgment to a poor night's sleep or being worried about an upcoming medical appointment.

Similarly, entrepreneurs disregard the high percentage of new businesses that fail. They believe that their situation is different, readily concluding that such a high failure rate couldn't possibly apply to them. Who would start a new business without believing that they would beat such terrible odds? The sheer number of new businesses that fail speaks to the optimism of entrepreneurs to wander down such a gauntlet, and their willingness to believe that norms don't apply to them. But on average, of course, they do.

We also apply representativeness in judging investment opportunities by comparing one investment to another. It's an easier task than to evaluate it on its own merits. Why go to the rigor of analyzing a security if it's similar to the other one that you owned before?

Suppose that you're familiar with a business that provides a service for small merchants to sell their products more easily on an internet platform, like Shopify Inc. (SHOP). Then a new startup offers a similar omnichannel platform. Its service enables users to manage an entire business, from inventory, customer preferences, sales, analytics, and orders, to onsite point-of-sale (POS) terminals. Instead of analyzing the new company from the ground up, there's a natural temptation to use the framework and assumptions already in place for the first business. By doing so, you'll be naturally influenced to see parallels between the two businesses that are oversimplified or may not even exist. You may be induced to think that the share price of the new company is set to rise as swiftly as SHOP did in the first few years since it became publicly traded. Instead of assessing a new company's prospects, we are lured to adopt the more manageable task of comparing them to another similar company's results.

Investors also favor quick-growing businesses with a willingness to pay higher prices for their rising earnings, often before such earnings materialize. This is especially true of new businesses with sexy stories about how they will disrupt the status quo. Anticipating how advancements will impact our lives and imagining the possible resulting profits doesn't replace sound fundamental analysis of cash flows and real business earnings. When trends occur at a fast pace, it isn't always easy to keep up with analyzing new options. Taking the easy way out and relying on comparisons can be an enticing alternative.

Using a proxy to draw a conclusion seems to be a sensible approach on the surface. Although no two companies, investments, or periods are the same, sometimes they rhyme. Relying on representativeness becomes problematic when we form conclusions from information that isn't as closely related to the comparison as we think, and we see patterns that aren't really there.

Consider an investor trying to decide how to allocate her RRSP contribution this year. She received two investment recommendations from friends. She lays each one-page summary on the dining table for comparison. The first recommendation is a portfolio of consumer discretionary stocks, including Amazon and The Home Depot – names that she is familiar with. The second is a diversified portfolio of emerging market investments – investments in countries that are not yet developed – that performed exceptionally well over the last year. Even if you don't know much about consumer discretionary stocks or emerging market investing, you may have drawn a quick deduction based on the headline information. This is representativeness in action: taking the small amount of information to draw broad conclusions.

Perhaps you like the idea of owning companies that produce familiar products, so the consumer discretionary portfolio is where you feel a higher conviction to invest. Maybe the word *diversification* attracts you to the second option, since you believe that you should never keep all of your eggs in one basket. Or perhaps you heard positive comments about emerging markets generally, or an encouraging report about discretionary consumer spending that entices you to prefer one option over the other. In any of these scenarios, you cannot possibly know anything about the merits of either investment by what it is called or the short description on the page – yet you'll be enticed to begin to develop a preference based on such limited information.

There is a reason that investment funds are required by law to warn that past results do not predict future returns. Partly due to representativeness, investors predictably rely on past returns as a proxy for expected growth, even though one year of outstanding growth is more likely followed by average or subpar returns. Similarly, generally good or bad past investment experiences with a particular stock, sector, or strategy will also persuade you to reinvest or avoid it regardless of its actual prospects. That is why the timeless adage warns us to never fall in love with a stock.

In another example, it is a commonplace error to conclude that companies producing quality goods also make quality investments. Quality manufacturing is a valid reason to buy their products. Relying on this experience to determine that the company's stock is also a good investment seems to be plausible on the surface. After all, there is a certain relationship between the goods a company produces and their prospects as a business. However, these two aspects are further apart than you may want to believe. If you adore a particular brand of clothing or make of car, that doesn't mean that the business's outlook is favorable or that the company's stock is a good investment. Harley Davidson makes very good motorcycles, but that doesn't dictate their economic outlook. Relying on aspects that seem to be related can lead to false conclusions – and poor investment choices – when they are not as closely connected as you think.

Representativeness is at the root of other investment analysis distortions, too. Imagine that we are trying to determine which business is more likely to be an oil resource company:

a. ABC Corporation has 500 employees and a net income of $600 million.
b. ABC Corporation has 500 employees, a net income of $600 million and its headquarters are in Calgary, Alberta.

If the headquarters of company B led you to believe that it is more likely an oil resource firm because Calgary is known to host a high number of these types of companies, you're experiencing representativeness. It is tempting to conclude that the second description better resembles – or represents – your preexisting belief about oil companies. Not only will you tend to feel more comfortable assuming that company B is a better fit, the more details that fit your preconception about oil companies, the higher your conviction in that evaluation will seem. Nevertheless, this is faulty reasoning. The more details provided, the narrower and more exclusionary the definition becomes. That is to say, the more details, the less likely (not more likely) that it is part of that group – oil resources or otherwise.

Representativeness can also dupe you into seeing an upward or downward trend in stock prices that isn't there.[3] Just because markets rise doesn't mean that they will continue to grow or that it is time for them to change direction, yet it is pleasing to see patterns from one period to the next. That selected period doesn't necessarily represent the longer cycle, yet it is comfortable and pleasing to see a pattern from one period to the next.

Representativeness is an efficient way to process quick decisions. Shortcuts are timesavers for a reason: They omit details that can differentiate a profitable decision from one that you regret. Tread carefully when making assumptions based on representativeness. If it walks like a duck and talks like a duck, it might not be a duck.

MONEY ILLUSION: The Rule of 72 and the Risk of Inflation

*the money you save
disappears quickly due to
compound inflation*

There is a simple reason why Canada doesn't mint pennies anymore: the cost of production and the value of copper are more than the face value of the actual coins. Five hundred years of relentless price increases have relegated this zeitgeist to the craft supply box. By using an epoxy filler, old pennies make a lovely do-it-yourself copper table-top! Even US pennies are now constructed primarily from zinc.

When the daily price of goods expands as imperceivably slowly as a melting polar icecap, it is easy to overlook inflation's destructive force. Even though we complain about the small difference in the price of a head of cauliflower, cost increases go largely unnoticed over relatively short periods. Since inflation is compounded, however, its influence is dramatic over the long run. Climbing prices rise exponentially because you pay for increases on the increases.

Between 1900 and 2015, the average annual inflation rate was 2.9% in the United States and 3% in Canada. The most extreme growth peaked around the same time just over 20% in the US in 1918 and over 15% in Canada a year earlier. By 1921, both countries experienced their most severe recession on record, with inflation dropping −10.7% and −15.8% respectively.[4]

Even at today's modest 2% target inflation rate shared by both the US Federal Reserve Board and the Bank of Canada, prices will rise by 64% after 25 years. Even a small increase in inflation can materially impact future prices. For example, 3% inflation will double expected costs over that same period.

As much as savers appreciate compounding growth, spenders fear it. While the rule of 72 is a simple way to estimate how long it will take for an investment to double, it is also useful to determine how quickly your expenses will increase. By dividing 72 by the rate of inflation, you can estimate the number of years it will take for expenses to cost twice as much. If prices rise at a rate of 2%, it takes about 36 years for costs to double, or at 3% inflation it only takes two decades. The higher the rate of inflation, the sooner you can expect to pay multiples of what you pay now. "Compound interest is the eighth wonder of the world. He who understands it earns it. He who doesn't, pays it," said Albert Einstein.

Compounding inflation isn't the only glitch that wreaks havoc on our good intentions to save. **Money illusion** is the conventional way to think about dollars and cents in nominal terms. We tend to look at the value of money as the number printed on the face of the bill rather than its relative purchasing power over time. This is also called its *real value*, meaning that inflation has been factored into the worth of the currency. The real value is what a dollar can be used to buy. A twenty-dollar bill today is worth more than the same twenty-dollar bill a decade from now because it can be used to buy more goods and services. This calculation isn't simple, however, which is part of the reason that we tend to defer to the face value when considering its value. Remember when you thought that a millionaire was rich? She still is, but much less so than in 1990.

Money illusion is also why your Uncle John still gives you $50 per year for your birthday. That's the same amount that he's given you since you were born, and it was a tidy sum of money back then. He still considers the sum generous when, in reality, you can buy much less with $50 today than you could years ago.

As you plod along earning income, the amount of your payroll typically increases over time, counteracting the rising cost of living. Calculating inflation is a moot point if your asset values and wages increase at the same relative pace or higher. However, when you retire and withdraw a fixed amount from your savings, the growing difference between income and expenses becomes much more worrisome. The natural tendency to disregard rising costs begins to cause problems. If the ever-increasing gap between income and expenses expands too far, retirees may be forced to withdraw more money from their savings than they had planned, or alter their lifestyles.

Recently, a young client asked if he invests $1 million earning interest of $80,000 per year, whether he could live comfortably for the rest of his life. Unfortunately, the $80,000 that the investment produces today will only be worth about $40,000 in purchasing power 36 years from now, assuming that inflation doesn't grow beyond 2% each year. A loaf of bread in 1980 cost seventy-three cents ($0.73). Forty years later, it cost $2.45. That's more than three times as much, even though the difference is calculated at a slight 2% annual increase. Even at a low inflation rate, the erosion of money can be catastrophic to your future spending power when compounded over long periods. A $1,000 expense will cost you $1,485 twenty years later.

The combination of money illusion and compound inflation is the most impactful risk to your retirement plan. Saving too little money to meet your future expenses is the greatest danger facing people deciding to leave the workforce. Ironically, investing in many seemingly safe investment options puts conservative investors at the greatest risk of declining purchasing power.

Building inflation protection into your financial plans inflates the amount of money you need to save by a startling amount. You can counteract this effect, however, by investing in assets that appreciate as the economy expands. Generally, as prices rise, the businesses that produce those products and services earn higher revenues. That, in turn, increases their profits. Higher profits drive up the price of the company's shares. When your investments grow, you can offset the erosion of inflation on your purchasing power.

Even investment regulators display the effects of money illusion when they label investments as safe solely because the principle is guaranteed, and the return is fixed. Yet, these investments often carry negative real returns (after inflation). Low-risk investments typically offer modest yields that rarely match the growing costs of goods and services. After considering taxes and inflation, investing in so-called safe investments can put conservative investors at risk of declining purchasing power.

Low return investments that guarantee you cannot lose the nominal amount invested aren't very safe at all when you stand to lose future real value. A $100,000 GIC will be worth less than $67,000 in purchasing power after only a couple of decades at a meager inflation rate of 2%. If you retire at 55 and live to age 90, your $100,000 of interest income will only afford expenses of $44,570 in those final years, not including taxes. Such a dramatic deterioration can materially alter your planned lifestyle.

Your budget may be substantially impacted if you also have unexpected healthcare expenses on top of the effects of inflation. To afford

$100,000 of income 20 years from now, you will need $148,595 of income in today's dollars, at 2% inflation. You'll need much more if inflation runs at a higher rate or if you need additional healthcare.

At 2% inflation, you'll need to save roughly $1.3 million, invested at 5%, to support 25 years of $2,000 monthly retirement income. If your goal is $10,000 per month, plan on socking away $2 million before you retire unless you have a pension plan or other sources to help meet your needs.

Retirees who have an inflation-protected pension plan are among the most fortunate since the increasing income curbs the effects of rising costs during retirement – but these defined benefit plans are rare. Even money purchase plans, which act more similar to a retirement savings plan, provide benefits to counteract biases. Since participation is often prescribed, it's almost impossible to intervene in this well-constructed income plan. In some cases, pension participation is an employment benefit that doesn't require participant contributions at all. Given the natural biases that can stall or disrupt investment commitments, pension plans are a lifestyle advantage for most people, especially those that offer the envious inflation-adjusted benefits.

Even though you realize that prices rise over time, calculating the compounded erosion of your purchasing power doesn't come naturally. The future real value of money is a concept that isn't easy to evaluate. To reduce the risk of underestimating what your money will be worth in the years ahead, use the rule of 72 for a simple approximation. Divide 72 by the inflation rate to estimate the number of years it takes for expenses to double, and you'll see how impactful inflation will be on your ability to buy what you want.

RECENCY EFFECT: A Clear and Present Danger

what happened last week
influences decisions
since it's top of mind

An important aspect of a good financial plan is to define the amount you need to save to reach your financial objectives. The plan accounts for a given target rate of return, the speed at which costs are rising, the date that you start saving, and when you'll need the money. Investors rely on these blueprints to adopt an appropriate savings plan and typically spend the rest. The sooner you begin saving, the better your chances to attain more wealth, with the added benefit of reducing the amount of contributions you'll need to make.

Regardless of your savings start date, reaching your goals is ultimately dictated by the accuracy of the plan assumptions – the rates used to make the calculations. Since financial plans cover very long periods, it only takes a small variance between the expected investment returns and the inflation rate to produce dramatic errors.

Conventionally, people rely on prevailing rates to proxy long-term results, focusing most heavily on current trends. Unfortunately, investors who earned double-digit returns recently are not only anchored to that experience when making assumptions about the future. They also tend to rely more heavily on recent experiences, believing that the current trends are most likely to continue into the near future.

This **recency effect** describes the natural inclination to apply more weight to current data, believing it to be most relevant. Retirement savings plans, investment portfolios, and even insurance policies project expected values several decades ahead. A plan can dramatically miss the mark when the estimated inflation rate is too low or the expected returns are overly optimistic. Adjusting your plan late in the game to avoid running out of money in retirement is painful.

Unexpected events that affect your savings – even over short periods – can also derail the timing of your planned retirement. Although the 2008 financial crisis was relatively short-lived, the considerable drop in asset prices forced many would-be retirees to rethink their arrangements. When interest rates and equity returns are substantially different than anticipated, you may be forced to postpone your plans. Or, in desperation, some investors opt for higher-risk investments despite the increased volatility and risk of capital losses. Neither of these strategies is recommended to fix a financial shortfall, especially for risk-averse investors.

In another example of how your expectations for investment conditions cause distress, the Canadian government unexpectedly altered the tax treatment of income trust units in the early 2000s. Formerly, investors had become used to receiving high distributions from these investments. After the change, income trust units almost disappeared, having lost their tax advantage. Investors who had come to rely on these high cash-flow securities began seeking riskier investments to produce the same amount of monthly income.

A conservative approach to long-term planning can mitigate some of these planning risks. However, choosing a lower projected rate of return than current rates illustrates our natural bias for the prevailing market experience. We are still tied to it, having merely adjusted from it. Adopting a conservative view relative to current rates is a step in the right direction, yet may still result in overstated projections due to our preference for recent market conditions and the anchoring bias discussed in the first section.

Even professionals have difficulty predicting substantially different conditions in the future than today's experiences. Practically speaking, it's almost impossible to plan for a wildly different reality due to our natural bias to think that the future will look somewhat like the present. For example, imagine if inflation suddenly spiked to 8% or 15% for a few years instead of the Bank of Canada and Federal Reserve's target 2%. Even if inflation rates eventually drift back to that lower level, your future costs will always incorporate the period of hyperinflation and can result in a savings shortfall.

The problem is easy to understand when you consider the GIC and bond yields of the 1980s and 1990s. When you are receiving a guaranteed return of 7% to 12%, it's almost unfathomable to imagine interest rates dwindling to near-zero by 2022.

In those days, clients renewed their maturing GICs in person, booking an appointment to meet with a personal banker at the local bank branch. There was no such thing as online banking in those days.

I was one of those bankers and can attest that almost unanimously, clients tended to prefer a one-year term paying 9% over a five-year term at 7.75%. They certainly didn't think it was wise to select the lower yield. But, as interest rates swiftly declined, it would have been better to lock in the lower rate for five years than renew annually at lower and lower yields. Like streamers on top of the sailboat indicating wind pattern changes, when long-term rates are lower than short-term rates, it's a telltale that trends are likely changing.

Similarly, for homeowners, the lowest-rate mortgage term isn't necessarily the ideal choice. When interest rates are rising, selecting a longer fixed-term may be more advantageous, even if the rate is initially higher than other options. It's alluring to choose the cheapest interest rate regardless of the term, partly due to the view that the future will be similar to the present. Often that is the best strategy, but not always.

Interest rates dropped from a peak of 21% in 1982 to almost zero four decades later (Source: Bank of Canada). With interest rates meaningfully suppressed by monetary policy makers today, depositors are responsible for reflating their savings with more of their own earned money.

By the middle of 2020, Canadian and US long-term investment-grade bonds paid investors less than a half-of-one-percent, a wide departure from the double-digit guaranteed yields a few decades earlier. With such modest returns, many savings plans are bound to fall short of earlier projections. Making matters worse, the bumpy ride for equities over the first decade of the 2000s produced long periods of poor overall investment growth.

Generally, people are slow to adapt to new experiences, even when the change is dramatic. To test this, try asking a real estate agent or investor about the risks of future price declines. Those who had the experience of earning hundreds of thousands of dollars flipping homes in recent years are quick to claim that real estate prices always appreciate. Yet, that wasn't the case over other long periods of time when interest rates were rising.

After consistent asset price growth, it's easy to find investors ready to dismiss the risks. Yet, the material risk of rising interest rates, tax policy changes, civil war, terrorism, or even a measly recession can dismantle the real estate market in short order. These legitimate issues are not as unlikely as many real estate investors beholden to the **recency effect** want to believe.

In the case of interest rates, many people thought they had hit bottom after the 2008 financial crisis. Yet, a decade later, interest rates dropped to new lows. Once interest rates are near zero, there is more room to rise than to drop, especially if supply chains disrupted by a pandemic don't heal quickly enough, or if workers are reluctant to return to work, creating wage inflation as employers offer bonuses and higher incomes to entice them back.

People are not blind to the fact that interest rates change or that the status quo isn't as constant as we'd like. Moreover, investors understand that dramatic economic shifts can take effect, especially over a long time-horizon. Yet, it would be difficult to make plans if we believe that calamity was just around the corner. It's easier to build decisions around predictable circumstances. It's simpler to believe that the most relevant proxy for tomorrow is today, so our future expectations are inevitably tied to what is happening now. Like many other biases, the recency effect goes almost unnoticed and is easily excused.

When considering your investment options, or even when you're renewing the interest rate term on your mortgage, look for signs that the landscape is changing. A shrewd borrower will guard against the beguiling effect of the recency effect by keeping leverage in check and not borrowing beyond what you can comfortably repay. Also, access to emergency cash or line of credit can smooth out unexpected financial events. It's also worth remembering that real estate is a long-term asset class, generally not easy to sell relative to more liquid investment options such as publicly listed and traded stocks.

REVERSION TO THE MEAN: That Makes Sense but Doesn't Answer Anything

the obvious cause
isn't always the reason
that explains the act

Consider the claim that smart women, especially those with the highest intelligence quotient (IQ), tend to marry men who aren't as bright as they are.

Is this a true statement? Are you now rattling through your mind to test this claim against your experience?

You likely have established views about women in general, and you may consider the variety of women in your life. Perhaps you hold an opinion that smart men prefer to avoid competitive relationships. Maybe a couple that you met recently comes to mind that resembles the scenario. In any case, your everyday experiences will come to mind that provides you with context to draw a conclusion about the claim presented at the opening of this section.

Let's leave the plight of smart women for a moment and examine another statement related to children. Specifically, this dramatic pattern relates to children who exhibit incredibly violent conduct.

Consider another claim: Children's extreme behavior tends to lessen after three months of taking a daily dose of ibuprofen. *Please note that I do not advocate or recommend any medical treatments and haven't researched this issue.*

If you don't have direct experience with violent conduct or with children, you may draw on other experiences. For example, you may naturally substitute the question about violent adolescent behavior with something that relates to what you know about ibuprofen instead.

Did you also wonder who reported these results and questioned their motives or their qualifications? After all, it seems like a very humble solution to remedy childhood rage.

In the last example, the statement will take on a much different topic to illustrate how we validate statements. This example is alarming due to the impact it can have on your wealth.

Investment funds that earn more than 10% in excess of the stock market index almost always suffer lower performance the following year.

What do all three of these scenarios have in common? Exceedingly smart women's selection of a male partner, the effectiveness of ibuprofen on extreme behavior by juveniles, and the performance of wildly successful investments are all examples of an extreme event. Since common examples happen more often, it is more likely that the next occurrence will be closer to average simply due to math.

Mean reversion describes how a radical example of an event is more likely to be followed by a less extreme example. Since average results happen more frequently than unusual ones, chances are higher that the next instance will be closer to normal. Average results happen more frequently than extreme ones.

Statistically, it's more likely a child with extreme behavior will act more normally in the future than not. Since the ibuprofen is the only notable factor provided in the story, you'll be inclined to believe that the drug influenced the children's behavior, when it may have nothing to do with it at all. Instead, the change of behavior is better explained by **reversion to the mean** because normal behavior is more probable. Also, since most people are average, the quantity of suitors with a lower IQ than the woman in vignette is greater. Since there are more of them, there are more to choose from.

Similarly, excessive investment results are also uncommon, and extreme market events are unlikely to recur despite our willingness to believe they will. It's also easy to look for causes to explain resulting changes in performance or market moves. However, extreme events often revert to the mean because average events are more likely to occur since they are more common.

AVAILABILITY BIAS AND DISTORTION: Overestimating What You Can Easily Recall

emergency kits
sell out at the local stores
after the earthquake

How much work do you do to maintain your home, including regular cleaning, weekly chores, and overall house maintenance? Take a piece of paper and write down the percentage of the work you end up doing most of the time. Then, ask someone that you live with the same question, and add the two figures together. If the result is more than 100%, you are experiencing **availability bias**. We typically overestimate experiences that are easy to recall. The effort you put into housework is always easier to recollect than the work done by your housemate.[5]

Not all memories are created equally. Some experiences are more easily retrieved – or *available* – in your memory bank. Events and facts are quicker to surface when they take place recently or when they have been repeated. We also tend to recall more emotional or dramatic events. You'll more easily dredge up horrific and startling incidents when the intensity of the event sears the details in your mind.

The ease with which you are able to recall information can also result in misjudging the frequency or magnitude of occurrences and their consequences. Have you ever purchased an emergency kit right after a natural disaster? Rushed to the store to stock up on flour, toilet paper, or medication that you wouldn't normally keep on hand right after a medical event like a heart attack, or during a pandemic? Easily elicited memories, however, are not a reliable gauge for the risk of recurrence. The proximity of an event and the way these memories dominate your mind just makes you think it does.

That is why you become a little reluctant about snorkeling in open Hawaiian waters after you hear a news report about a rash of jellyfish stings in Australia. Availability bias is the propensity to overweight the importance and likelihood of readily recalled facts, and then rely on this information to make decisions. This tendency can also skew your view on investment prospects or may limit your opportunities to profit.

Despite the thousands of stocks available, it isn't surprising that investors select the ones that catch their attention. Companies' share prices that surge or plummet sharply, or those that are highlighted on news feeds and social media, are often the first additions to an investor's strategy. For example, the popularity of publicly traded cannabis stocks when Canada and the US first began legalizing personal use of marijuana in the early part of the twenty-first century resulted in thousands of lost dollars for many eager investors.

Being quickly reminded of investment successes, failures, or extreme volatility can also affect your appetite for risk, and taint your views on the prospects of certain investments. Your investment choices are distorted through the voice of your experience, and the louder the narrative – the more recent or dramatic – the greater the influence it has over your seemingly independent judgment.

In one instance, a client instructed me never to purchase rate-reset preferred shares in his portfolio because he lost a substantial amount of money on them in 2015 when the Bank of Canada surprisingly cut the overnight interest rates. The dividends on these particular preferred shares are reestablished every five years, so lower interest rates translate to a lower dividend. Many investors who sustained a drop in the share prices and feared that interest rates would not increase by the next reset date sold them. Since preferred share investors typically seek to limit investment risk, the price drop was startling. A substantial number of investors abandoned these securities due to the dropping prices, possibly because they didn't understand that the price decline was due to an unexpected interest rate policy change, and not a deterioration in the quality of the investment. Nevertheless, preferred share prices remained low for several years until the prospects of rising interest rates regenerated interest in them. Then, these underappreciated securities rose dramatically.

Regardless, this particular investor could not come to terms with this type of security's ability to provide attractive tax-sensitive income and handsome profits once the interest rate landscape changed. From the bottom of the Covid-19 shutter in March 2020, rate-reset preferred shares, despite their significantly lower risk profile, enjoyed stellar returns only matched by the high-flying technology sector (Source: Refinitiv).

Easily retrieved memories will also lead you to believe that the recurrence of an event is more probable than it is. The volatility of the 2008 financial crisis and Great Recession was dramatic, but it is now well in the past. Yet, the recollection of the events and emotions associated with the significant unrealized or realized capital losses sustained by investors at that time still triggers a powerful reaction and can lead investors who suffered to take a more conservative stance than they would have otherwise.

The easy recall of these events is presumably to avoid past failures, but as in the example about preferred shares above, it can also result in overreacting or harboring an irrational viewpoint. You'll be tempted to believe the probability of a recurrence is more significant when, in the case of the financial crisis, the safeguards and regulations implemented by the governing bodies significantly reduced the possibility of a future repetition.

It isn't easy to let go of past experiences, nor is it wise. As the saying goes, those who forget their mistakes are doomed to repeat them. Nevertheless, be aware of the weight with which you view recent or extreme events, and the extent to which they influence your viewpoint. Once bitten, twice shy isn't a very good investment strategy. Axioms never replace the benefits of research, and are rarely helpful in evaluating the prospects of investment opportunities or dangers. Often, they are meant to be applied to a different scenario.

FAMILIARITY BIAS: Recognizing a Stranger

familiarity
may make you feel comfortable
inducing more risks

Have you ever looked over your investment portfolio and noticed that you feel more comfortable with the companies that you easily recognize? Have you thought of selling the ones that you were less familiar with, if they hadn't performed well? Or held onto companies with household names that provide services that you regularly use, even though the shares dropped in value?

More often than you'd like to believe, you'll be motivated to make investments for no other reason than your comfort with their general business, location, or even the products and services that they provide. You'll also tend to feel more relieved to sell stocks that you don't know well, especially when those investments lose value.

Take a look at your current investment portfolio. If you select your own securities, you may discover that not only do you carry a disproportionate number of companies that you're familiar with, but there's a good chance that more of your money is invested in sectors that you profited from in the past. Basing future investment decisions on past results isn't necessarily ill advised, yet it doesn't predict success, either. However, if you excuse investment concentration by telling yourself that your familiarity with domestic companies or specific sectors helps you understand those investments better, your **familiarity bias** is the justification for your familiarity bias.

In every case, concentrating your investments increases your risk unnecessarily. Moreover, if you've made your investment decisions primarily based on your familiarity with little or no investigation of the investment merits, or if you neglect the vast number of other opportunities, your bias has created an invisible governor on the profits that you can earn.

Meta Platforms Inc. (formerly Facebook), Amazon.com Inc., Apple Inc., Netflix Inc., and Alphabet Inc. (the parent company of Google) – referred to by the acronym FAANG stocks – became popular investments, in part, for being famous. In the same vein, investors have also driven up the share price of Tesla Inc. (TSLA) to 1,200 times its earnings in January 2021 (Source: Refinitiv). While TSLA is arguably a cutting-edge electric vehicle manufacturer and battery developer, 1,200 price-to-earnings (PE) ratio is indisputably an exaggerated price to pay compared to the average S&P500 stocks that historically trade around 16 times their earnings per share. Yet, investors continue to tout the merits of investing in these shares with no shortage of justifications.

It isn't difficult to imagine why you tend to prefer the shares of companies that you know or that dominate the media. It is easy to feel a false sense of security based on common knowledge. Consider, however, how *representativeness* – discussed earlier in this chapter – falsely urges you to think that a company producing quality products also makes a good investment choice. Producing superior goods may erode profits due to higher production costs or marketing expenses. Moreover, other business risks may exist that you hadn't considered. Without conducting an investment analysis, familiarity with a business is no more revealing about its investment prospects than representativeness.

Similarly, **home bias** – similar to **familiarity bias** – can influence you to buy the stocks of companies that operate in your geographic region because of your acquaintance with their operations or the economy that you and they both participate in. You may even find yourself defending a concentration of investment in your local region or country by reasoning that your understanding of resident companies or the native economy provides you with an upper hand over investing elsewhere. Regardless of the rationale, a disproportionate investment locally increases your risks by having too many eggs in one basket. It also limits you from a wider set of investment options.

Familiarity bias muddies your objectivity by repeatedly drawing you to the things that you believe you know best. Compounding this natural tendency to stick to what you are most comfortable with are the algorithms installed in many internet search features and elsewhere. These algorithms are meant to appeal to your interests, yet inadvertently keep you from finding new opportunities and insights. If you rely on such algorithms for your financial choices or if you tend to stick to the same news sources to formulate decisions, the effects of familiarity bias may be compounded by these features and technologies.

You may also find in your portfolio that you hold a meaningful number of shares of a company that you used to work for. You may even believe that you have insights into their prospects due to familiarity bias. One client told me that she would never sell her Telus Corp. (T) stock, despite the fact that she owned more T shares than any other investment. This point of view prevented her from diversifying her holdings.

She worked for the company for 30 years and the shares always performed well for her, she said. Despite having been retired for almost a decade, she felt that she could predict the trading range of the company's share price. On several occasions, she reported that the share prices would rise or fall within a certain price range without reviewing the company's earnings reports or any other objective data. Furthermore, whenever the price of T shares dropped, she enquired whether it made sense to buy more, even though it would result in further concentration of holdings, elevating her risk. Familiarity bias provided her a false sense of security when she was actively increasing her risk by investing primarily in a single investment.

Some people argue that you can eliminate foreign currency exposure by investing solely in domestic investments. That's true; however, in the case of Canada, it represents less than 5% of the world's investment markets and its economy relies heavily on resources. Those who limit investing within the country's borders are disproportionately exposing themselves to commodity prices and limiting the scope of investment opportunities. Also, today's marketplace offers participation in foreign economies without currency exchange risks by investing in domestically listed exchange traded funds (ETFs) with an internal mechanism for hedging the currency. There are also American (ADR) and Canadian (CDR) depository receipts, where global companies are listed directly on a US stock exchange or large US companies trade directly on the Canadian stock exchange with a currency hedge. Any of these products provide direct investment into a wide variety of foreign investment options. However, since they are listed on a domestic exchange, they offer certain tax advantages and the convenience of local trading.

Familiarity bias drags you to the safety of your comfort zone, and in so doing, unwittingly increases your risks by limiting diversification and investment opportunities. Countless bodies of research confirm that diversification is the key to consistently and successfully growing your wealth. The next time you're adjusting your investment portfolio, consider whether sticking to your comfort-zone is as effective as you believe.

PROPORTIONAL MONEY EFFECT: Why We Save Pennies Only to Neglect Dollars

cash is fungible
so why do we save pennies
and waste the dollars?

Unless you have a fondness for Sir John A. MacDonald or Alexander Hamilton, other than foreign exchange rates, the value of a 10-dollar bill is the same on either side of the Canada–US border, regardless of whose resemblance is embossed on the front. An old crumpled-up US cotton and linen twenty-dollar bill is worth the same as today's newly minted crisp twenty-dollar federal note. Contemporary Canadian polymer notes, with EURion constellations and watermarked design to make it difficult to counterfeit, stand up to a few more laundry cycles in the pocket of your favorite jeans. But that is where the differences end.

It is the interchangeable nature of money and the constant value of denominations that make it irrational to care about some dollars and not about others. Yet people are content to divide money into different buckets and to assign different values to them depending on where the funds originate or how you intend to spend them. This tendency is called **mental accounting**, which will be discussed in greater detail in the next section. First, we will explore the natural tendency to barter in relative percentages, disregarding the value of money during large negotiations and disproportionately hoarding small change during modest-sized transactions.

As a case in point, running to the store for a dozen eggs has become unnecessarily complicated. Grocers carry egg types that range from classic white, brown, Omega-3, vitamin-enhanced, free-run, free-range, vegetarian-fed, certified organic, and the lovely, colored shells of Araucana chicken eggs. Each label sells at a range of prices, starting somewhere near four dollars, climbing to more than double that. How do they determine the pricing for extra-large Omega-3 or small-sized vegetarian-fed blend?

It's easy to pace back and forth in front of the brightly lit cooler lined with glass shelves and soldiered rows of cartons. I realized that no matter how hard I press my index finger into my chin, it doesn't improve my ability to make the decision whether to splurge on the eight-dollar variety. Is it twice as healthy or doubly delicious, or is the price difference due to a free-the-chickens tax? Why do I hate to pay that much more for a dozen eggs, yet I can't bring myself to buy the cheapest carton, either?

Just buy the darn eggs that you want! It's only a $3.50 difference. Yet, because the most economical package of eggs is only $4.50, paying almost double the price becomes a mental hurdle. The proportional difference is the stumbling block.

"Take care of the pence and the pounds take care of themselves," is good advice. It should be, since it was first uttered by the Secretary to the Treasury of Great Britain, William Lowndes, back in the seventeenth century. The willingness to apply the advice to pennies and dollars today demonstrates our natural tendency to disproportionately focus on small quantities of money over larger sums.

> *"How much are you asking for that sweet '67 Chevy Impala?"*
> *The seller responds, "The powder-blue SS? It's easily worth $36,000."*

The haggling over the price of a car often ends with the buyer and seller settling on a nice rounded figure. People conventionally agree that haggling the trade down to odd numbers like $31,963.55, for example, isn't worth the effort.

Moreover, bargaining over the value of a car would take an excessive amount of time if the process started in pennies, nickels, or even quarters. It's practical to negotiate in larger increments and round numbers up or down when dealing with large transactions. Nevertheless, at the end of the negotiations, the flagrant disregard for dollars persists. People throw away the value of small denominations when the total price of the item in question increases. The higher the price, the larger the sum of money that negotiators are willing to disregard. This is the **proportional money effect**.

Since money is fungible – meaning that it can be used to trade for almost anything of its equal value – the efforts to save small amounts on small purchases is absurd if you ignore them during pricier transactions. $1.75 is still worth $1.75. If you become giddy to save $15 on a pair of pants, or buy two cheddar cheese blocks when they are on sale for $2 off the regular price, why would it be nonsense to care about saving $70 on the price of a $750,530 house? The proportional money effect describes the typical disregard for small sums during high-value negotiations and a disproportionate concern for these same small quantities when spending insignificant amounts.

Consider a settlement offered in a legal dispute. It would be ridiculous to ask that the offer be increased from $1,000,000 to $1,000,001.50. You'd be laughed out of the courtroom. Nevertheless, it seems reasonable to decide later that same day to splurge on a bucket of your favorite brand of double-fudge ice cream because it's on sale for $4.50 instead of the regular price of $6.

You may be thinking, "I don't sweat the small dollars anyway," and that may be true. Regardless, it is odd behavior to ignore smaller denominations when transacting high values since it is the large transactions that provide the most obvious opportunity to keep more of your money. The next time you're negotiating a contract or making a large purchase, remember that money is fungible, and saving on a single large transaction alleviates the efforts of squirreling away small sums over multiple trades.

MENTAL ACCOUNTING: Pigeonholing Money

cash allocated
toward wedding expenses
won't pay the car loan

Money doesn't care where it came from or where it's going. Its role is to store a value to be used at a future date. Frankly, it is simply easier than paying for stuff with chickens or other cumbersome goods that don't fit into a wallet.

All dollars are equal. Cash is exchangeable for items of equal value. It doesn't discriminate between trades with goods, services, or other financial instruments. The value of $100 is equal to $100.

So, if you treat certain money differently than other money, does that make you irrational? Surely, it's absurd to worry about one dollar more than another, yet we do it all the time.

Mental accounting is the natural bias to separate money into different categories based on how you attained it or where you plan to spend it. This bias can be advantageous when you apply it to set up your budget. A strategy to ensure that your basic needs are met first by funneling enough funds into a specific bank account to pay for important fixed costs – such as rent, mortgage, and utilities – is a wise step. However, when you set money aside in a holiday fund when you could use that cash to pay off credit cards or other non-tax-deductible debt, you may be causing more financial harm than good.

Mental accounting also becomes problematic when you naturally characterize money as distinct based on how you acquired it. Employment income, for example, is typically set aside for regular expenses and to do the heavy financial lifting. On the other hand, gifts and other unexpected money are swept into a mental account to be used for impromptu or variable expenses, such as treating yourself to a dinner out that wasn't in the plans.

You may be thinking, "Of course, that's natural because I work hard for the money I earn, but gifts are a treat." Money that's given as a gift is often segregated from the money that you earn. However, it's valuable to note that you can buy the same things with dollars from employment income as you can with money from somewhere else. Remember: Money is fungible.

Inheritance is a good example of how people assigned a unique quality to money due to how they acquired it. Often, estate beneficiaries segregate bequeathed assets from their other savings. You may feel inclined to treat gifts from parents or esteemed friends more carefully than the savings that you've accumulated from your direct efforts.

Sometimes these gifts come mentally preassigned with the tenets of the deceased benefactor. Some people find it difficult to detach from the sentimental value of a gift. Imagine that your conservative parents leave you $500,000, so you decide to keep those funds in a safe investment strategy because it's what they would have done, even though your other assets are focused on growth. There is also a tendency to use gifts to reduce debt – thinking it to be fiscally responsible – even if holding onto the loan for tax reasons or when leveraging is a more advantageous strategy.

In another example, suppose your father had invested heavily in oil and gas penny-stocks for most of his life. In that case, you may feel compelled to keep those shares that were passed down, even if they are not a suitable investment for your risk appetite, or when you haven't the faintest clue of how long or why he was holding onto them.

Most of the time, gifts from the dead don't come with strings attached, at least not effective ones. Even if the deceased intended to rule from the grave, it isn't an easy task. Generally, the giver wants the bequest to be helpful, and expects you to apply it in any way that provides you an advantage. Regardless, you will be inclined to isolate gifted assets from your other earned income.

Other windfalls, however, are often allocated to more frivolous expenses. If you've already set aside earned income to meet your budgeted items, it's natural to think of a windfall as an opportunity to spend on something that wasn't in the budget. After all, it isn't very much fun to apply a birthday card full of twenty-dollar bills against your outstanding credit card invoice or your car loan. That can feel more like punishment than reward because debt is caused by past spending that no longer brings the elation of something new. Even if you sold some old furniture on consignment, there is a tendency to put those extra funds toward nonregular expenses.

People hold a preference for current pleasure over future pleasure. It's rare that you'd consider contributing a windfall to your retirement savings plan, unless, of course, you purposefully allocate a proportion of all of money you receive to your savings and other important goals. Now, that's a good idea but not one that is natural.

The most peculiar example of mental accounting may seem like a windfall, but it isn't a windfall at all. Despite the clear advantages of holding onto your money as long as possible to invest or reduce debt, many people prefer a tax refund than to owe money to the government for the income that they earn each year. For example, in 2019, the Internal Revenue Service (IRS) and the Canada Revenue Agency (CRA) each reported that nearly 96 million US taxpayers and almost 20 million Canadians stood to receive a refund of overpaid taxes. In the case of Canada alone, the CRA controlled close to $37 billion in extra taxes owed to Canadians who overpaid.[6]

Taxes paid in advance and not yet due is the equivalent to a tax-free loan that you're granting to the federal government. It is your money all the while, yet you gave it to them early. Instead, you could have used it to invest for yourself to earn hundreds of additional dollars or pay down your debts to save interest expenses. The missed investment income on the money owed to Canadians in overpaid taxes invested at

4% was a whopping $1.48 million in 2019. If you expect a tax refund, it is because you remitted too much for the income that belonged to you all along.

Another ill of mental accounting is the stickiness that funds have to where you allocate them. Imagine that you're planning a wedding and have set aside $5,000 for the bride and groom's attire. When the gown and tuxedo end up only costing $4,300, how do you feel about the $700 that you saved? Would you be more willing to apply it as an unplanned mortgage payment or put it toward the wedding reception? If you're like most people, once the money is in the "wedding budget," that's where you're more likely to spend it.

If you diligently save for a holiday and the plane tickets cost less than you expect, you may be inclined to upgrade to your hotel, plan an extra excursion, or bring the extra cash along for spending money. Excess holiday budgets are rarely redirected to reducing your line of credit, fixing the house, or topping up your savings plan. Yet those are each valuable use of the funds to help you reach your goals.

Money doesn't favor where it came from or what it is spent on, and neither should you. Negotiating a lower lease rate for office space doesn't produce a different kind of wealth than you'd earn with a raise. Mentally assigning money for a specific purpose can be helpful to ensure that you attain specific goals, but be prepared to comingle funds from different sources and for various purposes to generate the most fiscally beneficial outcomes. It isn't natural, but it will save you interest costs and compound your asset values.

ENDOWMENT EFFECT: Loyalty Reward Points Are Not Free Money

we tend to value
our possessions higher than
what others will pay

It was a retail shoe business in Battle Creek, Michigan, in the late 1800s, where Shelley Byron Hutchinson came up with an enterprising idea. If customers were given a collectable token that could be exchanged for discounts on future shoe purchases, they might be enticed to keep coming back. The scheme was so successful that he elicited the financial backing of Thomas Sperry, and together the two built the first independent trading stamp company.

By 1986, the Sperry and Hutchinson Company began rewarding shoppers with stamps at gas stations, supermarkets, and the general department stores. Squares of paper were doled out to consumers based on their purchases at participating stores. The stamps were given away for free, incentivizing consumers to patronize the shops with stamps over those that weren't participating in the program. The Green Stamps were perforated, dry-glued on the back, and issued in denominations of 1, 10, and 50 points. The value of each stamp was nominal, but, when licked and pasted in the complimentary 24-page collectors' books, a family could amass up to 1,200 points with a full binder. Surely, you'd buy a jar of Pomade hair elixir at a store that gives you bonus stamps instead of one that doesn't, as long as the selection and price for the hair wax is similar.[7] The collection process was easy and engaging. Consumers came to attach value to what were called the S&H Green Stamps, even though were free. And so, loyalty rewards were successfully launched due to their appeal to shopper's biases.

One such reason for the appeal of free points, is due to the **endowment effect**. People tend to value their possessions higher than others are willing to pay to acquire it. The sense of ownership and an aversion to losing something that you possess seems to evoke this experience. For example, if you're given a selection of rooms to set up your new office, you'd likely be flexible on which one to select initially. But, when you are assigned a specific office, once you adopt the decision, you'll feel more reluctant to trade for another one. Researchers have tested this bias with everything from coffee mugs to real estate and found the same sticky results regardless of the item at hand.[8]

This phenomenon helps to explain why people are reluctant to part with their belongings. You may be inclined to believe that your belongings are worth more than even you'd be willing to pay for the same item if you didn't own it already. The effect is even evident in goods that were initially free of charge.

There is also a natural allure to acquiring something for free, whether you need it or not. Imagine strolling down the aisle of your favorite grocery store, pushing a metal buggy full of your regular grocery items, when you're offered a free sample of dishwasher detergent. You will likely accept the free sample even if you don't own a dishwasher. You can always give it to someone who does, you may rationalize. Despite being free, there is an intrinsic economic value for the soap, but the bias to endow value on the free item is intriguing nevertheless.

Muriel Billes understood how valuable loyalty was in 1958, when she, the wife of one of the founders and first president of Canadian Tire, inspired Canadian Tire money. With roots planted back in 1922, the company had discovered the attachment people have to a small token of value. It is a compelling proposition to receive the free notes to later redeem toward purchases.[9] Canadian Tire money became so popular that other retailers accepted the pseudo-currency as a cash-equivalent to avoid losing customers. Today, consumers need to establish a Triangle Rewards membership with the company, which still provides a nominal cash value for the store's patronage. Albeit nominal, there is an intrinsic monetary value attached to the points, coupons, and stamps awarded, since you can save money on future purchases.

You'll also tend to keep track of accumulated reward point worth in one of your many mental accounts, thanks to your predisposition to segregate windfalls based on how you acquired it or what you expect to spend it on. Loyalty points, including stamps, coupons, or other trade-able awards are not as fungible as money, but are flexible enough to contribute to the cost of a wide variety of purchases. Yet, because we feel as though we didn't earn the points (in the same way that we earn our paycheck) people are more willing to squander loyalty rewards or use them toward nonessential expenses. Easy come, easy go.

Due to these effects, it is difficult to disregard or throw away loyalty tokens, even though they were free in the first place. People prefer to spend the vouchers even if that requires outlaying more money as part of the transaction, rather than tossing them in the trash. With mental accounting and the endowment effect working in concert, people predictably prefer to use the points, spending money to do so, rather than not. And, while some reward systems can amass to large values, many are nominal. Even a fifty-cent coupon is difficult to toss out if it's redeemable for something you'd likely buy anyway, even if it means shopping at a specific store.

By the mid-1900s, S&H Green Stamps were ubiquitous. Everyday folk were licking and sticking squares of paper into the pages of the S&H

stamp-collection booklets until they were heavy and falling apart at the binding. With the exceptional success in North America, the company grew to overseas markets. It issued Pink Stamps in the United Kingdom since another company had already trademarked green stamps.

It wasn't until the recession of the 1970s that the stamps' nominal value was no longer enough to induce spending, collecting, and the loyalty that went along with them as people tightened their belts. Despite the system's demise, the lessons of the profitability of loyalty programs were not lost.

Loyalty schemes have come a long way since the turn of the twentieth century. With the compelling nature of loyalty rewards, and the fact that most consumers now carry a smartphone equipped to follow the value of point systems automatically, it's easy to see why so many retailers offer such programs. They are enticing, easy to track, and quickly adopted. Loyalty rewards programs today are as simple as downloading a smart-phone application and scanning the Universal Product Code (UPC) or Quick Response (QR) code whenever you make a purchase. These programs are essentially the same as the S&H stamps from hundreds of years ago, but digitized. The rewards are not designed to save the consumer money as much as they are intended to ensure that you spend in specific ways, on a particular brand, or sooner then you planned to. Also, the contemporary electronic tracking provides retailers with data insights into your spending habits.

Merchandizers realized decades ago that a sale price is naturally tempting due to anchoring, discussed in the beginning of this chapter. Of course, a shrewd shopper would rather spend less for the same item. The allure of a sale, however, goes beyond buying what you need at the best price. A lower price for a limited time encourages you to make the transaction right now, whether you want the item now or not. It can also lead you to consider buying goods and services that you don't need at all.

A relatively new phenomenon with online shopping attracts shoppers to automatic, scheduled purchases for items that they regularly consume. Recurring purchases also shortens the spending cycle and promotes more frequent buying patterns since consumers no longer rely on their memory. When you establish a recurring purchase of dish soap, the usual distractions of your busy life don't interfere with your regular spending. That is something that retailers are pleased to see, and they are willing to provide a modest incentive to earn your committed purchases. The retailer has the added benefit of knowing that you won't pick up a bag of cat litter at another store.

Marketers appreciate the influence that sale prices, coupons, and loyalty reward points have on your spending decisions. They ultimately use these schemes to influence how and when you spend money, with a preference to expediting how quickly money leaves your wallet. When you feel that you are being cajoled into purchasing something you don't need now or maybe don't need at all, you likely are. You often see through these tricks; nevertheless, avoiding the temptation of these schemes is often more complicated than you realize.

Whether you decided to collect loyalty rewards on your credit card, with your travel provider, or from your grocer, they are never a constant value. You can realize better value by spending the rewards in certain ways or for certain goods. It's no accident that there is no standard calculation to value points. To understand what each point is worth, you'll have to investigate various ways that the points can be traded for goods and services, and many of them now have an expiration date. Loyalty rewards have one goal, and it isn't to increase your wealth.

The value of points is only what you can trade them for, yet it's typical to hoard them for a rainy day. Counteract the tactic by spending the rewards on items that you would normally purchase with cash. Find the best advantages that you can obtain from them, with a reasonable amount of investigation without letting the complicated accounting to value each point bog you down from using them. It's better to spend them to save more of your cash. It's always better to have more money than more points any day of the week. Cash stores value longer and is more flexible than reward points.

When you cannot use points toward what you need, and to use them requires additional capital that you hadn't planned on spending, consider donating the points instead. You may receive a tax credit for the donation if the value is substantial enough and useful to the organization. And, even though loyalty rewards tie you to a specific retailer or set of goods, they carry a monetary value, so don't forget to list points in your will.

STATUS QUO BIAS: The Influence of Inertia

the more choice you have
the wealthier you may feel
but the less you act

In act 3, scene 1, of *Hamlet*, the protagonist contemplates the pros and cons of life and death. "To be or not to be – that is the question," he ponders.

Hamlet is a hopelessly ambiguous man. His never-ending assessment and revaluation of every choice prevents him from taking any action. As he sets out to avenge his father's death, he first comes across Claudius kneeling in prayer. Hamlet convinces himself not to slay the man in such a vulnerable state, fearing that it would cause Claudius to ascend to heaven. Then, Hamlet creates doubt by questioning whether the ghost of his deceased father was a devil sent to manipulate him into seeking revenge. He further throws himself into debate by wondering whether he should rise above the barbaric action of murder altogether, believing himself to be a thinker rather than a slayer. Hamlet's indecision and self-imposed muddling ultimately prevents the execution. He just can't get the job done.

Spoiler alert: Hamlet doesn't avenge his father at all. However, by the final act, all the main characters are dead, as all good tragedies should end.

Hamlet's circular reasoning prevents him from acting. When doubt arises, it delays your ability to come to a decision. When you don't have all of the details or you're unsure of the end result, a lack of clarity makes choices uncomfortable, often suspending the process altogether.

And, when you don't know what to decide, it is easier to keep doing what you are already doing, which sometimes means doing nothing at all. Maintaining the **status quo** is less conflicting than to decide to change course. It also takes less effort.

Cloud storage plans and software services, for example, profit from the number of people who no longer need or want their service but don't cancel the plan. Subscription companies understand that opting out of an automatic payment plan is just as much work, if not more, than subscribing in the first place. When the monthly cost is modest, it is easier to continue paying for something that you don't want or need than to spend the energy to figure out how to stop it.

It is also easier to delete an unwanted email than to unsubscribe from the email list, despite realizing the sender will keep spamming you with more messages in the future that to ponder and delete. That's for the future-you to worry about. It's the path of least resistance.

Even highly motivated people set decisions aside when unsure of which direction to take. Effort can also complicate a decision process when the workaround or a *rule of thumb* isn't readily available, and no easy solution emerges. In some instances, choice overload and choice-confusion are to blame for postponing or avoiding decisions. The **status quo bias** takes over when we abandon a decision and keep doing what we are doing. The passive approach wins more often than we would like.

Economists theorize that we should be happier with more choices. The more options you have at your disposal, the better. You can be more precise given more alternatives, right? Instead of being given blue or red, imagine that you have a color wheel with teal, cobalt, azure, navy, crimson, candy, berry, ruby, or brick. The added hues should be beneficial.

For many people, however, added selections confound the choice instead of enhancing it. Imagine that you have a 12 × 12 foot room that you're planning to paint. It's an expense of both money and time, and you don't want to waste either one on the wrong color. Blue or red is a cut-and-dried choice, and easier than agonizing over the shades and hues of 14 various tones. The difference between red and blue is more comfortable to resolve than evaluating your preference between subtly different palettes labelled *deep garnet*, *Georgian brick*, or *raisin torte*.

The fear of making the wrong choice can also prevent you from making any decision at all. Choosing the wrong paint color is one thing, but it isn't the end of the world. In fact, if the dizzying number of paint chips doesn't stall the process, it's likely that you realize that the out-come, even if wrong, isn't going to affect you for long. You can just get another bucket of paint and set aside another weekend.

When it comes to finance, however, consequences are more mean-ingful. That adds pressure to the process, which may upend an already complicated choice. Avoiding financial decisions is common, but detri-mental, when delays cause consequential loss. You may not realize that the loss of time is a financial forfeiture. Due to the effect of compound interest and the time value of money, the status quo bias decreases your future wealth.

Consider private pension plans, deferred profit-sharing plans, and other employer-sponsored investment compensation packages. In addition to offering these plans for the benefit of employees, some companies even offer to match the employee's contributions. The number of new workers who neglect to complete the paperwork to begin the program is surprisingly high, even though these plans offer substantial benefits to all who participate. The amount that the company is willing to match is equal to earning a 100% return on your contribution! The obstacle standing in the way is reportedly being unsure of the quantity to invest, and which investment options are best. This has been recognized by behavioral economists as so prevalent, there is a movement to provide opt-out plans instead of the common opt-in plans. Now, many employers are offering that option to their employees with an automatic basic enrollment.

Even when your contributions to a savings plan are relatively small, delaying the commencement of an investment plan is surprisingly costly. A $100 monthly contribution may only amount to a measly $1,200 by December. However, one year later, at a 6% return, that $100 monthly contribution matched by the company results in a worthwhile sum of $2,467.11. Forty years down the road, however, that single year of missed contributions will be worth $25,376. You would only have contributed $1,200 from your paycheck to have an extra $25,000.

Suppose you contribute $300/month when you're 30, assuming an 8% return, you could anticipate a nest-egg nearing $690,000 by the time you're 65, and you will have only contributed $126,000 of your own capital. If you delay saving until you are 45 years old, you'd have to put away $1,170 per month to make up the difference. Instead of contributing $126,000 from your income, you'd end up contributing roughly $280,000 to end with the same value at 65!

Literally, time is money. Starting to save now instead of later lessens the amount you will need to contribute to any savings plan. Adding funds earlier result in fewer contributions overall to achieve the same results due to the power of compound interest. Status quo bias is worth fighting. If you don't have a professional advisor or someone you trust to help you decide, arrange the contributions to your pension or savings plan as quickly as you can get them started. You can always amend your contribution plan later.

Chapter 2

Controlling Risk

CONSERVATISM: Close but No Cigar

*your view of the world
doesn't always price-in all
new information*

As circumstances change, people naturally resist new information and tend to rely too heavily on existing beliefs and earlier decisions – especially when those views worked well in the past. You can probably think of everyday examples where people hang onto old ideals, even to their detriment. Past fashion trends felt great to wear when they were in style but can look out of place or even gauche years later. Or when salespeople continue to rely on formerly successful gimmicks, now tired and ineffectual, over more astute consumers in the current environment.

It's difficult to change, and when we do, we typically take a stepped approach rather than a wholesale change. Instead of adopting new views completely, you'll likely combine both old and new information into a hybrid opinion. **Conservatism** describes this typical reluctance and may cause you to adjust your existing opinions and anchors insufficiently when presented with new, different data. Frankly, it feels like a safer strategy to incorporate new evidence in a middle-of-the-road approach rather than adopting it in its entirety, even when accepting the new information fully provides a more accurate perspective.

49

Despite the seemingly conservative approach of holding onto former beliefs – even parts of them – this reluctance can hamper your financial views and dilute the effectiveness of your choices: that is to say, this seemingly conservative approach can limit your financial results and expose you to unnecessary risk.

Take, for example, when a company issues an increased pace of earnings growth. Especially when this type of news comes as a surprise, shareholders and new investors will typically consider the report with a grain of salt, failing to react sufficiently. It's typical to attribute the unexpected growth to an isolated event rather than a sustainable change in the company's growth pattern. This preference is unilateral and this conservativism results in a dampened enthusiasm for otherwise prosperous news. As a result of the hesitancy, the stock price will remain undervalued.

The reverse is also true. An unexpected decline in earnings is just neglected as often as an upside surprise. Under the guise of this bias, you'll find yourself rewarding companies for their historic growth for far too long. By acting with caution and skepticism of the new decline, investors are too slow to accept the deceleration growth. We prefer to favor former opinions about the company's capabilities and reward companies for historic performance long after it has dwindled away. Earlier reports continue to impact your opinion of the company's prospects even after it has begun to decline. Ironically, this conservative approach leaves you exposed to further downside risk.[1]

When most investors act conservatively, the collective response (or unresponsiveness) can leave stocks mispriced for a surprisingly long time. The share price is dampened or propped up by investors' common reluctance because stale information is still incorporated in the decision to invest.

However, being in front of such a trend can be profitable. Instead of going along with the crowd of investors naturally subject to conservativism, consider earnings reports critically and be prepared to freshen your outlook. Other investors are subject to these biases too, so don't look to the crowd to substantiate your point of view. When the pace of earnings increases or decreases – especially when it takes the market participants by surprise – don't be shy about believing the report.

An unbiased investor will buy any investment at an undervalued price, profiting from the difference. It's also shrewd to sell securities that overstate the company's prospects. Don't be fooled by conservativism. There's nothing safe about harboring old beliefs. Comfortable assumptions from the past may be more persuasive than you give them credit, and share prices are persistently higher (or lower) than warranted.

GAMBLER'S FALLACY: Heads or Tails?

average odds
aren't a real-life example
of a single chance

For every flip of a coin, the chance to land on heads or tails is equal. Yet, when the coin lands on heads several times in a row, you'll likely feel compelled to predict that the next flip of the coin will land on tails. The more times in a row that the coin lands on heads, the more your confidence in calling tails will grow, even though the odds for each coin-flip have not changed.

People are bound to the belief that results should more or less resemble average odds. Out of 50 flips of the coin, its common to think that about half will be heads and half will be tails. Yet, it's just as likely that they will be all heads or all tails. Random flips of a coin do not need to represent the average, and they often don't.

Imagine that you flipped a coin 50 times, 45 of which landed on heads and 5 on tails. The odds of landing on heads on the next throw aren't higher because of earlier results since each flip of the coin has an equal chance of landing on either side. It is just as likely that the coin lands on heads half of the time as it is to land on heads every time.

The earlier results have no effect on the next flip of the coin. There is no causal relationship between the coin toss results.

Randomness doesn't have a pattern, but it feels like it should. This is called the **gambler's fallacy**. Even if you are tempted to dream up a string of random coin-flips in your mind, you will likely predict more variety in the number of heads or tails than would result if you actually tossed the coin in the air. You'll be drawn to feel that randomness looks more jumbled than the patterns that usually happen in actual, real-life samples.[2]

Randomness looks more like a pattern because we assign it meaning. However, there is no causals relationship between random events, including the toss of a coin. Nevertheless, it's more comfortable to believe that randomness has a pattern. When you think can anticipate or predict pattern changes, you'll feel a greater sense of control over your environment, which in turn provides peace of mind – even if you've manufactured this belief.

When it comes to investing, you'll also yearn for patterns. Random events influencing stock prices lead you to believe that the next move is understandable, if not predictable. After a string of days that the market drops in a row, you may be tempted to believe that it will turn up soon. Or you may harbor the belief that it should drop again for a few more days. In both cases, the illusion is that there are patterns in random events when none exist, because one doesn't cause the other.

Many of life's events are unsystematic – meaning that they don't happen according to a plan. Yet, you will still be tempted to find shapes and configurations. You'll naturally pine for formulas and trends to explain what is happening, and reach for markers to understand events. More importantly, you'll want to use these markers to define the future. It is more comfortable to envision a sense of control than to throw your hands in the air and let a random undefined reality wreak havoc.

When investing, the gambler's fallacy will falsely inspire you to see patterns and to think that you are able to control risk by timing the market. Timing the market is a biased investor's game. When you have a long-time horizon, your best option is to remain invested and disregard market gyrations.

POSSIBILITY AND CERTAINTY EFFECT: A Bird in the Hand Is Worth Two in the Bush

large wins are tempting
even if chances are slim
when the cost is low

> *"An old man turned ninety-eight. He won the lottery and died the next day. It's a black fly in your chardonnay. It's a death-row pardon two minutes too late. Isn't it ironic?"*
>
> *– Alanis Morrissette*

The famous Canadian singer-songwriter, Alanis Morrissette, knows what makes people tick. The internationally released album *Jagged Little Pill* won five Grammy Awards, including Best Album of 1995, of its nine nominations. The album later went on to be produced as a Broadway musical.

Her mezzo-soprano voice streamed through the Walkman's foam earphones of portable cassette and disc stereos and across the radio airwaves of the early 1990s. Her emotionally charged lyrics speak to an era of people, young and old. Even today, her Facebook page has more than three and a half million followers.

Morrissette has made a career of connecting to the inner hopes and dreams of everyday folks living their lives by striking a chord that runs deep. You could say that she wears her heart on her sleeve, and in later years, she reinforced that by writing a public apology to her former boyfriends. She has swallowed more than one *Jagged Little Pill*, and with it, she embodied some of the most heartfelt emotions that people share.

You don't need exclusive insight to understand the tragedy in the opening 14 words of her hit single, "Ironic," at the top of this chapter. The story's protagonist hit the jackpot of financial euphoria at such an advanced age, only to enjoy it for less than a day. Morrissette takes less than two bars to drag the listener from joy to tragedy. Sudden death is tragic enough, yet dramatically more song-worthy when it happens the day after winning the lottery. It wouldn't have held the same impact if the character in the song died the day after a great new job offer. Winning the lottery is the ticket to monetary freedom and happiness, only to be reversed within hours to the ultimate worst fate.

Is winning the lottery all it's cracked up to be? After all, "winning the lottery" isn't a phrase strictly applied to lottery outcomes, but is now broadly applied all sorts of unexpected good news. However, does it warrant the amount of happiness that we have always assigned it?

Most of the fun of playing the lottery is imagining a debt-free life and the liberty of an unabashed buying spree to follow. Toying with spending an amount of wealth that most people will never see in their lifetime is a fun pastime. Anyone who's played the lotto has spent at least a fleeting moment picturing their name on the cartoon-sized check at the lotto center. Perhaps you've imagined the phone call telling friends and family that you plan to share it with them, or informing your boss that you won't be coming into work tomorrow...or ever.

Anticipating a joyful event releases a brain chemical that induces the sensation of joy, regardless of how unlikely the occasion may be. With odds of 13,983,816 to 1 of picking the lucky six numbers out of a possible 49, you probably won't win the lottery. That doesn't diminish the pleasant psychological effect that the neurochemicals in your brain induce when you consider the prospects of a mountain of cash and how your life would change if you win. Winning the lottery is so unlikely, however, that more joy comes from imagining the prize by everyone who buys a ticket than the unique experience of the single winner.

Isn't the small cost of the ticket worth the little piece of imagined joy? With the cost of a ticket so low and the prize relatively enormous, the allure to take your chances on such an outcome makes the gamble enticing. And yes, there are biases involved.

The **possibility effect** is why lotteries and weekend trips to Las Vegas are wildly popular. The amount you wager is small. If you don't win, you haven't lost much, and your level of regret is minimal. In the case of a weekend in Las Vegas, it's easy to justify the gambling costs as part of your holiday entertainment budget.

The small wager is so enticing that you would likely regret playing if the ultimate winning ticket is from a local store or someone you know. You wouldn't want to be the only person at work that didn't participate in the office lotto-pool in the unlikely event that they hold the winning ticket. It would be even worse fate if you forget to buy a ticket the very week that your own lucky numbers are drawn. And so, for an insignificant token, you can eliminate the chance – albeit extremely remote – to feeling remorse.

Also, buying a ticket increases your chances of winning from nothing (with no ticket) to a small chance. That's a material difference! You've created the possibility to win a giant sum for a very small cost. Merely increasing your chances if you already have a small chance, is ironically uninteresting to most people. If everyone held a 15% chance to win, increasing your probability to win to 20%…or even 30%, it is far less enticing. In both cases, you increase the odds by a small amount, but by moving the possibility from zero to any amount is more compelling than the same incremental increase if you already have a chance to win.

These decision patterns are not only consistent with playing the lottery, but are also evident in a common desire to limit the risk of an unlikely event. Whenever the cost is small and the risks are significant, people are inclined to participate – even if the hazard is extremely rare.

When you worry, it's uncomfortable. Avoiding pain – even the anticipation of pain – is highly motivational. That is one of the reasons that people book vacations in advance rather than waiting to find a last-minute deal. It reduces the uncertainty that your plans may not turn out, causing regret. It is comforting to spend a little more now to secure your trip rather than take chances that your dream vacation plans fall through because you waited for a last-minute price drop.

Insurance works in a similar way by converting an unlikely financial catastrophe to one with limited costs. People purchase protection against all sorts of rare disasters with the objective of buying peace of mind. The natural tendency to prefer certainty over a variable outcome, despite how remote the possibility, is called the **certainty effect**. Most people prefer to receive $30 for sure rather than have an 80% chance to receive $45, but a 20% chance to be left with nothing. Nevertheless, the second option has a higher calculated benefit and a statistically higher output ($45 × 0.8 = $36). If you were unbiased, you'd opt for the second choice.

If you could convert a likely outcome to a certain one, you'll probably feel more comfortable. Instead of waiting for events to unfold, fear of regret stands in the way, even when you stand to gain a higher reward by waiting for the result to unfold. Anticipating the ache of regret if the odds don't play out as expected can impel you to play your hand prematurely. This is why a plaintiff in court can feel like settling for a reduced award rather than taking their chances in the law process. A bird in the hand is worth two in the bush.

Creating certainty – something calming in an unstable situation – removes negative emotions, usually with a limited financial cost. Creating possibility – something exciting when none exists – generates positive feelings seemingly out of thin air, also at a cost. These are both powerful motivations that regularly erode your wealth. When you consider it in that light, you may be more critical of your decisions to lock in certainty or gamble on possibility. You may also want to stop to contemplate if the emotion that you're after is worth the price.

It is wise to cover the risk of major economic perils to sustain your financial security, even if the risk that they will occur are small. However, if you're paying more for a holiday to avoid disappointment (loss) or settling a court case for a diminished award, ensure that you are content to spend your money to avoid negative emotions. They are just feelings and they may or may not be worth the price. Similarly, if you enjoy glee in an evening in Las Vegas, it's wise to keep your stakes in line with the benefit of the pleasure.

HOUSE MONEY AND BREAK-EVEN EFFECT:
What Just Happened?

you may double-down
even when you want low risk
to conceal losses

The intimidating pitmen pace the roped-off area just beyond the gaming tables keeping a keen eye on the players. The roulette wheel spins in a blur. And, the lit sign above the playing area displays the last eight winning roulette numbers to taunt casino patrons to try their luck. Given our general predisposition to see patterns when none exist (gambler's fallacy discussed earlier), the number-series persuades players to think that they may have a better chance than the actual odds of those cheering at the table.

In roulette, players bet on the single numbers ranging from double zero to 36; rows of numbers; or numbers between 1–18 or 19–36. They may also choose the color of the numbered squares (red or black) or bet whether the winning number will be odd or even. Naturally, the most unlikely gamble comes with the highest payoff. If the ball lands on the single number corresponding to the square on the table where you've placed your bet, you'll reap a stunning 35 times your stake. $10 becomes $350. $500 becomes $17,500. Not a bad score!

Bets that come with a higher likelihood pay a significantly lower prize. If you guess the correct color or when the winning number is odd or even, for example, you'll only win twice as much as you wager. The higher probability to merely double your money makes the larger wager seemingly worthwhile.

Despite the rarity of winning at roulette, the popularity of the game suggests that a 35 times payoff is enough to keep players at the table after losing multiple times. Casino are not foolish businesses. Incorporating a zero and double zero slot on the roulette wheel ensures the odds are squarely in the casino's favor.

If you play roulette for entertainment, you can extend the time at the table by playing both the low-odds/high-payoff game and the high-odds/low-payoff game, simultaneously. Placing the same wager on individual numbers as you do on the outer game to double your money, at least you'll get back the full amount that you play almost half of the time.

Nevertheless, after you win a game of chance, or once your investment increases, you can reduce your risk by taking your initial money off the table or selling some of the investment. When investing, especially if you're speculating and you're unsure of the investments merit – you may feel that it's prudent to withdraw your original investment and a portion of the profit. Your initial investment or wager is now safely back in the bank.

In the case of a night in the Las Vegas Strip casinos, you may think to slip the chips that you started with back into your left breast pocket for a pleasant surprise later. If you're like most people who use this strategy, you may feel that you didn't lose any money, but don't fool yourself. Even if you come out even at the end of a night of gambling, you still gave up all of the gains that you lost in play. You will prefer to mentally net-out the gambling wins and losses for the day or the week rather than see them as a series of wins and losses.

Imagine that you come out ahead after one day of gambling. In that case, you'll likely feel that the money you won is the house's money – not really belonging to you yet. Whether gambling or investing, if you profit quickly and easily, you will tend to keep the gains in a separate mental account. So, if you subsequently lose it, you won't feel as upset as if you lost your original capital. Yet, they are both pots of currency.

This illustrates the common disconnect between your money versus your winnings – the **house money effect**. Gamblers and investors alike often separate the initial capital from profits in mental accounts, treating these pools of money differently, viewing quick profits as less important and money that you're more comfortable losing.

The house money effect is a bizarre dissociation from the truth that money is fungible. While gambling or speculating with someone else's money at stake is much easier because you feel that you have nothing to lose and everything to gain, doing the same thing with your own money is curious. The false belief that any profits were not earned or don't belong to you makes it easier to accept unnecessary or inappropriate risks.

Imagine that you're in a competition to select an exchange traded fund (ETF) in a fictitious online trading account. The person who selects the ETF with the greatest growth over six months wins a prize. You'll naturally select the most aggressive option with the most upside opportunity regardless of the risk because the investment isn't real money. If the investment drops to zero, you stand to lose nothing. Simulated trading accounts don't provide a real sense of investing, either, since the investor has very little fear of loss, since they have no money at stake. For the same reasons, after making quick returns on an investment or a bet, investors are inclined to take chances they would not ordinarily take.[3]

Your willingness to accept risk is also altered by losses. When you lose money on an investment, you'll naturally become increasingly reluctant to make additional investments, even when the opportunity is unrelated to the loss. After a loss, gamblers similarly feel tempted to reduce their stakes, even though the odds haven't changed.

A notable exception, however, is when you're offered an option to recover the loss. The motivation to **break even** is so tempting that you'll even consider taking more risk than you'd typically accept. If you've heard the expression "double or nothing," you've seen this bias in action. After losing a bet, the offer to double your money and reconstitute your original wager is extremely appealing.

You'll also be persuaded to hold an investment that has lost value for the express purpose to make back the lost money rather than seek profits in a new investment strategy. Even if a different investment option offers better prospects, you'll tend to favor the old investment over the new one. Starting over seems to *reset* the starting marker for gains and losses, and any losses on the new investment are considered a second failure rather than part of the first mistake. It feels better to make one mistake than two, regardless of the total quantity lost.

Although these effects are easily illustrated by the wins and losses in gambles or stock trading, consider your intuition in other scenarios. Imagine how you might feel when the value of your retirement savings account drops $17,000 in December. Come January, how ready or reluctant do you feel to add more money to the plan? When your investment value has increased over the year, however, contributing more money feels more comfortable. The rise in value is reassuring that you made the right decision to invest.

Ironically, lower stock prices and ETF unit costs allow you to buy more shares. Yet, people are not emotionally hardwired to buy after investments decline. Your natural feelings dissuade you from making prudent decisions for your long-run investment goals. The price deterioration causes you to pause and second-guess whether to add more funds to the strategy or to wait until you see evidence of a rebound. If the plan is sound, however, the lowest price is your best opportunity to buy more shares or units with the same amount of capital. It's just emotionally difficult to execute.

Sometimes a price decline reveals deterioration in an investment. In that case, reviewing an investment strategy is a good idea. If the approach doesn't fit your values anymore or if the investment's quality has changed, a different approach may be a better idea. However, when the price change is the sole reason for selling an investment or creates reluctance to invest more, you are likely making a mistake.

Both the house money and break-even effects illustrate how wins or losses temporarily alter your views on risk. Ideally, your risk appetite should remain relatively stable. Yet, your most recent experiences prod you to accept uncharacteristically higher levels of risk. You're more inclined to make a new investment after having success on your most recent transaction. You'll also feel more willing to accept risk when only your gains are at stake and your initial investment is safely off the table. Furthermore, it is tempting to accept high-risk options when you are offered a chance to regain a previous loss.

To best avoid the temporary changes in your risk appetite due to the house money and break-even effects, define your risk tolerance, as well as your ability to sustain losses, and write these important guidelines down. It is a good way to refresh and recalibrate your investment decision. You'll find tools available later in this book to help you do that effectively.

DISPOSITION EFFECT: The Worst Time to Lock in a Profit

selling your winners
while holding onto losers
is a common plan

When you decide to sell a stock, presumably, you believe the company will perform poorly in the future. Why else would you sell it? Yet sometimes, investors sell stocks for reasons that have nothing to do with the prospects of the company.

When you look at your investment portfolio, it's natural to feel good about the securities that have risen. In fact, you may be tempted to sell the positions that have performed well, thinking it's a good idea to capture the gain. After all, the "buy low, sell high" axiom tells you to do just that! However, the only reason to sell an investment is if you believe that it will drop in value, the investment is no longer suitable, or if another investment offers a better prospect – not to capture a gain and the positive emotions that go with that.

It's obviously unpleasant to acknowledge a bad investment decision and sell a security that has lost value. To remedy the pain of loss, you may be tempted to hold onto securities that drop, hoping that they'll make a recovery, rather than sell them to cut your losses and select a better prospective investment. Generally, you'll be motivated to sell sound investments and hold onto bad ones because you'll prefer to feel good about your gains and avoid the pain of acknowledging loss.

Selling your profits to lock in gains is a symptom of the **disposition effect**. Ironically, investments that appreciate are more likely to keep performing well, while poor investments – the ones you're inclined to retain – are apt to continue to lag. On average, winning stocks tend to produce better returns than the future returns of the losers.[4]

Even from a tax perspective, there is no incentive to sell stocks with gains. In fact, the opposite is true. Selling stocks that rise is punitive. As soon as shares are sold, the taxes on capital gains are due. The longer you hold the position, the longer you defer the taxes owed on the profit.

Whenever possible, reducing or deferring a tax payment is a prudent strategy. Yet, we are more likely to sell stocks that rise in value than those that drop.[5] This tendency is so strong that the disposition effect is one of the most robustly documented facts about individual investors' trading behaviors.

Of course, you have excuses to justify these decisions. You may be thinking that you want to give the laggards a chance to regain their earlier value – a bias tied to anchoring and the break-even effect discussed in Chapter 1 and earlier in Chapter 2, respectively. And, as you'll see in an upcoming section, loss aversion is also a compelling motivator to hold onto losing investments. When you sell shares that have dropped in value, you crystalize a loss. However, capital losses can often offset other capital gains. You can also carry capital losses forward to offset future gains made on other investments.[6]

Moreover, you can benefit from selling poorly performing investments that are no longer suitable so that you can reinvest the capital in better opportunities.

It is undeniable that selling securities that have risen for no other reason than to capture a gain is counterintuitive due to expected future profits and tax expenses. Although a confounding choice, familiar sayings such as "taking profits is never overrated" illustrate the commonality of this blunder.

Despite this clear evidence, the natural behavior is easy to understand. Simply put, you will likely favor the decisions that make you feel good and avoid those that are uncomfortable. However, when considering a change in your investment strategy, it is often prudent to consider selling the losers first. They offer the best tax advantages and often the best chance to improve your portfolio's outlook.

It doesn't matter what you paid for an investment. If it no longer suits your objectives or has poor prospects, you should sell it. Never sell quality investments that have a continued positive outlook no matter how tempting it is to capture a capital gain.

LOSS AVERSION AND FALSE RISK CONTROL:
Ante Up!

avoiding losses
even when you increase risk
helps to avoid pain

The house money and break-even effect are not the only influences over your decision to accept higher levels of risk. Your risk tolerance can dramatically change when you face episodes of financial loss. While your decision to keep an investment that drops may seem perfectly logical at the time, it's often counterintuitive and driven by hidden internal influences.

Avoiding the emotional distress of loss is such a compelling motivation that it can hijack your decisions without your consent.

The inclination to accept more risk after your investments grow is understandable. The house money effect can play a role in that. So can your desire to confirm that you're making prudent financial choices, as you'll read more about in Chapter 4. Also, due to the recency effect discussed in Chapter 1, you may believe that the current growth environment will prevail. The success of earlier investments offers compelling reasons to keep investing.

Ironically, however, you are also biased to increase risk when you are facing a sure loss.[7] Some investors even harbor the delusion that if they don't sell the stock when it drops, they haven't lost anything. Instead of seeing the decline and dealing with the negative emotion of loss, they may shift their attention to the number of shares – which hasn't changed – instead of the market value, convincing themselves that the share price can reclaim earlier values. This is a perilous position to take when investments decline in value because of a deterioration in quality. Cutting your losses is a prudent strategy to reduce your risk, but your bias could persuade you to hold the risky position, or even to buy more in a strategy referred to as *averaging down*.

Cutting your losses and reducing your risk is emotionally unpalatable, even for risk-averse investors. **Loss aversion** compels you to stay the course with a losing investment, even when it increases your jeopardy, is no longer suitable, or better prospects exist. You'll want to believe that the investment can regain earlier values, and in the process, increase your risk.

A few years ago, an accountant referred a client to buy Canadian flow-through shares to reduce his income taxes. The accountant suggested the strategy to reduce his client's $27,000 tax bill, which he viewed as an impending loss to his finances.

Certain Canadian mining and resource companies qualify for tax benefits from their exploration and development costs. These companies can pass the tax credits on to the investors who buy their shares. Since the investment in these corporations is highly speculative, the companies use the tax credits as a sweetener to entice investors. In many cases, the tax deductions are so hefty that an investor can deduct almost the entire cost of the company's purchase from their taxable income.

This particular fellow was seeking to eliminate his entire tax bill. He viewed the taxes as an unpalatable loss and was willing to consider available strategies to eradicate it. Both he and his accountant were inspired by the belief that the tax credits from flow-through shares could provide an opportunity to retain some or all of the money owed.

Given that his income was over $200,000, his marginal tax rate was about 50%. For every new dollar that he earns, he remits half to the government coffers. So, to eliminate the $27,000 tax bill, he would have to reduce his income by double that amount and invest $54,000 into the flow-through strategy.

Speculating is not for the faint of heart. Typically, the market value of flow-through shares is expected to drop. However, when the tax savings are considered, the overall advantage of the scheme can be profitable. On the other hand, these investments can dissolve just as quickly.

Investing $54,000 into the strategy would provide enough tax credits to eliminate his tax debt, which he was keen on doing. But the reality is that he was risking $54,000 to save $27,000. In managed flow-through investment pools, the portfolio managers who buy a collection of these investments mitigate the risk of an individual company going bankrupt by investing in several at a time. Notwithstanding, these speculative investments are highly volatile and carry the risk of permanent loss of capital.

Faced with the perceived loss owed to the CRA, it is normal for even conservative investors to become risk-seeking, as noted earlier. In this case, the man explained that he was a cautious investor, which is why he wanted to reduce the tax bill in the first place. Instead of cutting his losses and paying the tax bill, he was willing to risk double the amount due to loss aversion.

If you're naturally a risk-taker and your tax rates are high, risky tax strategies are sometimes suitable in limited quantities. If you're risk-averse, you're better off not jeopardizing additional assets, as oddly comfortable as it may feel when influenced by certain events. When you're facing an unrealized loss, the goal to cover the loss may induce you to take on more risk. Nevertheless, this is the moment to ask whether your goal is to increase or limit your risks. The existing loss is often less than what you're wagering to make it back.

Chapter 3

Wanting to Be Right

OVERCONFIDENCE: We All Can't Be Above Average

overconfidence
is not a good replacement
for quality work

When asked, most people believe that they are an above-average driver. We also tend to think that we are more amiable than the average person on the street, and we feel that our sense of humor is better than most. Yet, it is mathematically impossible for everyone to be above average.

People are also inclined to underestimate how long it takes to complete a task, but not how long tasks will take other people to complete.[1]

We are predisposed to believe that we are unique; that our individual case doesn't represent average experiences. Yet, each unique case is how averages are determined. Consider the following example of a critical health diagnosis with a limited statistical survival rate.

A doctor's role in providing life-changing diagnoses is critical. When receiving emotional information, patients are less likely to remember parts of the information due to the emotionally charged and sometimes complicated information. There are many unknowns, doctors often reminded patients, playing to the normal tendency to believe that individuals tend to believe that they can beat the odds of a negative outcome. Our hope overrides mathematics.

Framing is also important. The doctor could deliver the diagnosis of a particular cancer by indicating that 84% of patients dies within five years. Instead, she can provide hope by stating that as many as 16% of patients live beyond five years. In both cases, the risks are the same, but the second rearranges the facts to work with our brain's natural tendencies. Most patients will reason that they are most likely part of the 16% survival group. Statistically, patients believe their odds are better than average. This belief also provides a sense of influence over the outcome.

You may be unique, but so is everyone else. Averages are the mean of all unique circumstances. You're also inclined to overestimate your abilities, underestimate your risks, and exaggerate the amount of control you possess. It's normal.

You'll also want to attribute sound decisions to your skill and bad choices to luck or circumstances. Generally, you'll display an unrealistically rosy view of your abilities and prospects.[2] **Overconfidence** is the quality of excess confidence beyond your abilities. It is the belief that we are better than we actually are, and it plays a pervasive role in many aspects of our lives. These include investing, negotiations, and other financial decisions.

The number of transactions that take place on the stock exchanges is staggering. In every case, one investor thinks that buying is the best decision, and the other holds the opposite point of view. If you're ready to sell the position, shouldn't I be reluctant to buy?

As with overconfidence in our driving abilities, traders necessarily must believe that their reasons to buy or sell provide a superior conclusion than those of the person on the other side of the trade. In a case where both the buyer and seller believe they are correct, the most apparent reason for excess trading is overconfidence.

In the spring of 2020, preferred share prices in Canada had plummeted along with most financial securities around the globe when Covid-19 struck the hearts and minds of investors anticipating the economic disruption of stay-home orders. Normally, preferred share prices are tied to prevailing interest rates, as well as the credit quality of the company issuing them. Investors are generally willing to pay higher prices for preferred shares of companies with better financial stability. Also, as interest rates rise, these securities prices also rise because the dividends are based on prevailing interest rates.

With the economic impact of shuttering people at home, it was widely anticipated that central bankers would reduce the overnight interest rates to help stimulate the economy during the Covid-19 recession. Fear spurred investors to sell all kinds of securities in favor of the safety of cash. These motivations drove the price of preferred shares down to shockingly low prices, well below their $25 face value.

Due to the price drop, some of these quality investments paid investors fixed dividends near 10% relative to their share prices. Resolving to buy them is one thing, but finding large quantities of them available to purchase is another since there are only a few issues in the market compared to the high accessibility of large, publicly traded stocks. Therefore, sizable orders are managed directly with a designated trading desk that seeks to fill each order by searching the various public markets, dark pools, and institutional relationships.

After I had produced one of these orders, the trading desk called me. An institutional client was offering to sell a large position of one of the preferred shares I was interested in accumulating for my client's portfolio. She asked whether I'd take the full quantity of what the other trader was offering to sell. I paused.

I had spent hours researching the trade and validating my investment decision. Suddenly, my confidence dropped when I realized that someone else wanted to unload a substantial quantity of what I wanted to buy. There was a pit in my stomach. I had to consider whether I had done enough research, whether my biases were influencing my decision, or if I was wrong.

There are many reasons to buy or sell an investment position beyond biased reasoning. Selling shares doesn't necessarily mean that the investment is terrible either. For example, an investor may want to capture a capital loss for tax reasons or switch to another asset class for tactical reasons. They may be facing a margin call to cover loans secured with securities that have dropped. There are several legitimate reasons to sell an investment even beyond its future prospects.

I collected myself and set out to review my investment selection process and reasons to buy the position. Ultimately, I confirmed the decision and rationalized that perhaps one of their clients needed to raise cash for one of these other purposes. They didn't necessarily need to sell this preferred share because it wasn't a good investment, I reasoned. Regardless, I was on one side of the trade, and they were on the other. Neither of us knew why the other was making the trade. Both of us were unequivocally committed, believing that it was a sound investment decision.

Overconfidence is when you reliably judge your abilities beyond your actual skills, which can lead to investment errors, for example, when you feel good about a transaction that you could have spent more time on.

The ability to make investment decisions is essential, and understanding the market is a critical skill for investors who manage their own portfolios and investment professionals or analysts who affect the wealth of others. Similar to the self-assessment of our driving skills, most investment professionals believe that they possess above average analytical skills compared to their peers. Yet, not everyone can be above average. Both savvy investors and investment professionals are prone to overestimate their ability to read market conditions and make investment decisions. In short, overconfidence is common, and it can wreak havoc on investment decisions. Ironically, the more **overconfident** we are, the less we tend to believe that **overconfidence** affects us.

Evidence of overconfidence arises as a false illusion of control, deceptive beliefs about how quickly you can finish a task, or even an overestimation of the likelihood that a favorable event will come to fruition. Fear helps to slow down the investment decision process and provides additional reasons to check the foundation of your choices.

Take your time to apply a structured decision process to all financial decisions including investments, contracts, and other important aspects of your economic health. Overenthusiasm to see a project begin or overconfidence in your abilities can result in regrettable errors in judgment. In the following chapters, you'll discover processes you can apply to your financial choices to reduce the impact that overconfidence can play in your decisions.

HINDSIGHT BIAS IS CONVINCING: I Knew It!

the signs are so clear
that we feel we should have known
even though we couldn't

Have you ever found yourself muttering, "I knew that was going to happen!"

The phrase *20/20 hindsight* speaks to the impression that you could or should have predicted an event after it has taken place. Feeling that you understand the past feeds the illusion that you could have predicted it if only you had had all the facts at your fingertips. In retrospect, it's easy to see details that would have revealed the future if only you had paid attention to those cues! Yet, the reality is that you made the best decision you could have, given the information you had available.

In January 2018, Met Life Inc. (MET), a large US insurance company, surprised investors by postponing its earnings report. If that wasn't warning enough of trouble ahead, it also discovered an accounting shortfall. MET anticipated that it would need to set aside a half-billion dollars to remedy the error. Immediately, the share price dropped 10% (Source: Refinitiv). Later that day, I called a friend who held shares of the company. When she answered the phone, I could hear that she was upset. She admonished herself for not selling the shares a few days before, especially since she had considered doing so just a few days earlier.

Thinking that you could have anticipated developments puts you in a painful situation. Believing that you should have avoided losses or profited from news invariably leaves feelings of regret, even when there's nothing that you could have done differently. It still hurts.

This investor felt remorse for not having sold the MET shares prior to the drop. Although she could not have anticipated the accounting news, she blamed herself for not selling the shares before the announcement for other reasons. Either way, she was disappointed about how her inaction resulted in a loss. If MET's announcement hadn't occurred and the share price had held constant, her inaction would have gone unnoticed.

Not only was she subject to **hindsight bias**, but something else was at work. She hadn't sold the shares sooner because they were trading lower than the price at which she had bought them. Her purchase price was her **anchor**, and she didn't want to realize the loss, demonstrating **loss aversion**. She reasoned that the shares had traded at the higher price when she bought them and therefore, could return to that price, without any factual evidence about the financial prospects of the company. Essentially, she was hoping the share price would recover and save her harmless of the loss. She could not see that they were already trading at a fair price, so her bias prevented her from selling the MET shares days earlier.

One former client used to claim responsibility for profitable stock trades during a bull market, yet blamed losses on outside forces. He regularly asserted that he never trades stocks when the market is dropping. "I just sit and wait it out," he'd proclaim. This thinking preserved his outlook that he is responsible for the capital growth but that market declines were not his fault. This helped him manage the angst that comes from losses and the pain induced by loss aversion and hindsight bias.

The feeling that you could have predicted an event after it happens is natural. It's also referred to as the *saw-it-all-the-time effect*. We think we could have anticipated the past. We are also inclined to believe that we can predict the future with similar accuracy. Many times, this backward-looking clairvoyance results in overconfidence. When we overestimate our knowledge or ability and underestimate the risk, we host a delusion of control that doesn't exist.

No one wants to feel the discomfort of losing money. It's unpleasant. Paradoxically, hindsight bias punishes you for losses that could not have been anticipated.

It is easy to see how this sense of dominance over our environment is helpful for your survival. Without a sense of control, the sobering reality that much of life is random would leave us in a perpetual state of fear. In any event, coming to terms with the fact that market events are not known until they happen is refreshing. Share prices react so quickly to news that you cannot sell an investment before the price changes because no keen investor would buy them at the price you want to sell them – they've also heard the news.

While losses are painful, don't hesitate to dispose of investments that are no longer suitable, regardless of the price that you paid for them. Move past the unhelpful feelings of regret as quickly as you're able. With the vast number of opportunities on any day, there is undoubtedly a better option to increase your wealth than holding onto a poor investment.

COGNITIVE DISSONANCE: The Grapes Were Sour Anyway

you may fool yourself
to justify your actions
even when you are wrong

In one of Aesop's infamous fables, a fox eyes some tantalizing grapes. When he realizes that the vine is out of reach, he decides that they aren't tasty after all – without even placing a single grape in his mouth. Instead, he adopts the belief that the low-hanging fruit on a vine that he is able to reach is the tastiest.

This story exemplifies how you will change our minds to reduce **cognitive dissonance** between what you do and what you believe. You may initially think that you align your behavior to match your decisions; however, the opposite is often the case. You regularly manage your opinions and attitudes to feel good about your actions.

In the mid-century, Leon Festinger first proposed the theory of cognitive dissonance following experiments in which participants changed their views about a situation to justify their actions. He found that people prefer to alter their opinion rather than feel uncomfortable about behaving in ways that contravene their mindset.

In one of his experiments, participants performed a mundane task. Then they were asked to explain this boring assignment to a new set of recruits. Each participant was randomly offered either $20 or $1 as payment to convince the newbies to perform the task.

You may assume that participants who were paid $20 had a greater reason to lie to the new recruits. They were incentivized to lie by the higher payment! It may also seem obvious to think that those who were paid only $1 would tend to be honest about how tedious the assignment was. A dollar is hardly motivation to lie about the nature of the task. It isn't worth recruiting new participants for such a measly payment, especially if it takes dishonesty to cajole them.

Ironically, the opposite was true. Participants who were paid only the dollar felt a need to alter their perception about the task instead. They came to believe that the task wasn't so boring after all, so they could proceed with the job of recruiting. They changed their minds to avoid cognitive dissonance, the conflict between what they believe and how they act.

Cognitive dissonance affects investors, too. If anyone could anticipate a market drop, no one would ever invest in the market above the level to which it will decline. That is to say that market corrections are unforeseen events.

If you've convinced yourself that a market correction is likely (your belief) to justify holding cash rather than investing (your action), you may be under the influence of cognitive dissonance.

Suppose you're motivated to sell your investments, believing that you are taking prudent steps to protect assets from falling market prices. Then suddenly, the market dropped. How do you feel? Justified, no doubt! Nevertheless, timing an unforeseeable event is more likely a stroke of luck than skill or clairvoyance.

How would you feel if the market had risen dramatically while you were holding cash-equivalent investments, and you hadn't participated in the profits? One such investor soothed themselves by reasoning that there would be a price-drop soon and they would reinvest their capital then.

A bear market is measured as an index's decline of 20% from the highest to the lowest price. A market correction, however, defined by a 10% drop, is a relatively regular occurrence. Just because a stock market correction is regular doesn't mean that the next one is around the corner. Nevertheless, investors justify their decision with statements to help them feel better about their actions – or in this case, their mistake of missing out on investment profits. It is as though they want to believe that their decision was somehow correct, or will be corrected in the near future.

We have all heard prognosticators decree an impending market drop or other investment forecast that, in the end, doesn't transpire. If holding low-returning cash-equivalent investments results in disappointing returns while the market continues to grow, cognitive dissonance may be at work. Formulating a false story to justify your fears may make you feel better, but it isn't a successful investment strategy.

The best way to mitigate this scenario is to set out your investment strategy and maintain it. Unforeseen events are exactly that: unforeseeable. And timing the market is for biased investors.

CONFIRMATION BIAS: Buying and Selling a Boat

when spending money
you may be convinced to buy
and again, to sell

A scientific approach aims to find contradictory evidence to challenge what we believe. If you cannot find a way to dispute a fact, it is likely true. **Confirmation bias**, however, is the natural inclination to do the opposite. You'll have the tendency to look for, favor, and recall information that supports your point of view instead of challenging it. People have a natural tendency to rely on a validation process, rather than try to dispute our beliefs. This bias is so dominant that you will naturally be inclined to disregard information that goes against your outlook.

It feels better to be right than to be wrong. So, you'll prefer to find reasons to support the choices you've made instead of spending time and energy challenging them. But is that ensuring that you've made a good decision, or instead satisfying yourself of the decision that you've already made?

Consider how you make decisions and the process that you undertake. For example, imagine your decision about a major expense that is higher than usual or beyond your planned costs. How much effort do you spend talking yourself out of the purchase? Once you've made the decision, you're more likely to spend your energy justifying it. For arguments' sake, imagine that you're buying a boat, even though this same process can apply to many other types of financial choices.

Viewing or even test-driving boats is a safe margin from owning one, so taking a craft out for a spin is easily justified as harmless. After all, it's an opportunity to fulfill a dream for a short while without commitment. It may even be justified as a brilliant strategy in thrift, as well as making the most of life in one fell swoop!

At the helm, your wrist balances atop the wheel, leaving your fingers dangling effortlessly toward the touchscreen dashboard. Aviator sunglasses suck back onto your face by the jet-stream peeling over the windshield, randomly parting your hair as it whips and twists behind you. The positive experience certainly supports potential ownership.

You prop yourself up on top of the captain's chair seatback, turning around with a Cheshire Cat grin as the hull skips over the rollers. Your friends and family who came along for the ride are gleaming back at you. They unanimously give you the thumbs up, answering your teeth with theirs, and everyone resoundingly commits to spending every weekend with you wake-surfing, skiing, and tubing, further confirmation that buying a boat is a good idea as your imagination wanders off to an enhanced future.

You'll have so much fun. It will probably change your life. You've decided that you'll call these the boating years.

Once the decision to buy the boat is made, all that's left is to sanction your decision. The list of the improvements to your future family life is already drafted in your mind. Wisely, you set out a budget for fixed costs for gear, moorage, depreciation, and insurance, and amortize that over the next 10 or more years that you expect to own the boat. That fits within your **mental account** for vacations once you mentally borrow a bit from the entertainment budget. The variable costs for gas and maintenance are also within reach. There's an earnest belief that other pastimes will gladly move aside for summer boating fun. Giving up the snow ski pass for a few years seems like an easy choice. Change is good, you reason, and you've never really been fond of the cold anyway. All of your arguments support your decision, and you ultimately take delivery of the pristine Mastercraft wake-boat, complete with ballasts, touch screen operation, and some high-end cans to pump out the tunes.

Then, as seasons pass, each sunny weekend that the hull bobs in the lake, or rests quietly in dry-dock, comes with a small stab to the heart. Far too often, the weather doesn't cooperate or the gang has other plans. You even concede that those other expenses didn't stop as swiftly as you thought they would. Then another idea suddenly hits you.

If you sell the boat now, you can pay off the boat loan! You can go skiing this winter and take that trip that you've always wanted. Besides, the kids are growing up now and they have other interests. These are valid reasons to sell the boat.

If only you could have thought of the negative aspects before you spent all the money in the first place. Confirmation bias explains how the two happiest days in a boater's life are the day you buy the boat and the day you sell it.

In the 1960s, cognitive psychologist Peter Cathcart Wason conducted experiments known as the Wason's rule discovery task. The teacher thinks of a simple mathematic rule using addition, subtraction, multiplication, or division. Then the students begin to deduce what the rule is by presenting strings of results until they are confident that they understand the pattern.

For example, the student may ask whether 10-20-30 fits the teacher's rule – a second set of numbers that they believe fits the profile. If you think that the rule might be to count by tens, you may present a combination of numbers that confirms the pattern to increase your confidence. Once the student is satisfied that they know the rule, they reveal their conclusion.

The second set of numbers that you will present will almost always attempt to confirm your guess. In this case, you might have thought of submitting 60-70-80 or some other combination of counting by tens. Virtually no one would naturally try a result that discredits the rule that you suspect. People tend to think it's a waste of time to prove the thesis to be wrong. Why start from scratch to test a new rule when we have already made headway toward a solution?

The quickest way to ratify a solution, however, is to try to discredit it. When you're unable to refute it, the conclusion is more likely. We don't like to do that, however, because disconfirming what we already believe feels uncomfortable, and we prefer to avoid negative emotions. Regardless of how uneasy the feeling, your financial decisions will be better tested if you spend time critical of your beliefs by using reframing or by listing counterarguments.

You can easily talk yourself into and out of any decision, whether buying a boat or a house, choosing a particular investment professional, or allocating assets to a specific strategy. Confirmation bias interferes with good decision-making by seeking facts to support your view, when instead, it would be more valuable to consider the opposing view.

If you're convinced that an investment decision will be profitable, you are naturally attuned to notice supportive details, even dismissing countering facts. The danger is that you'll miss important reasons not to avoid the transaction, and may miss alternative options. In this case, a good way to calibrate your view and make better choices, is to create a pros and cons list, focusing effort on the cons, of course.

Try to write twice as many discrediting reasons as you have supporting ones. It will be challenging. After all, thanks to the conformation bias,
you likely have a long list of reasons that confirm your choice at the ready.

AVAILABILITY BIAS, RECENCY EFFECT, AND REAL ESTATE: House Prices Always Rise, Right?

what you remember
plays a significant role
in what happens next

Lord Harold Samuel wasn't the only surveyor working after the fall of
the Third Reich, but he was one with a unique vision. World War II air
raids destroyed over a half-million homes in the United Kingdom. The
rebuilding efforts could only produce a small number of the homes needed
to replace those lost in the war until Lord Samuel decided that redeveloping
bombsites was a good idea. He was right.

With his success, Samuel soon became a real estate tycoon and ultimately coined the notorious phrase, "Location, location, location,"
now considered a tested truth in real estate. While supply and demand
are the drivers of price, Samuel showed that real estate is a unique
commodity. Land is stationary, unlike most tradable goods otherwise
defined by size, quality, and style. By developing unwanted bombsites,
he demonstrated that almost all other property attributes can be altered,
as long as the location is desirable enough to warrant it.

Tracked by the S&P/Case-Shiller US National Home Price Index,
US home values rose more than 200% from January 1999 to 2022. Over
that same time frame, the Teranet-National Bank Home Price Index™,
tracking Canadian home prices, rose more than 300%. Notably, price
appreciation doesn't include rental income, or acknowledge that most
families leverage their home purchase by taking out a mortgage. Having
only a portion of your money invested in any asset amplifies the returns
on your investment. It's no wonder that staunch property investors
believe in the continued prospects of real estate.

The **recency effect** and **availability bias** divert your attention
to what has happened most recently. We naturally overweight our
opinions and decisions with information that is easier to recall, and

presumably, more relevant. Availability bias is a mental shortcut that relies on examples that are easiest to remember. This is the most efficient method for making choices, and it comes naturally at the neglect of other memories and data that is less handy.

It isn't surprising that people rely on their experience to form their point of view, having updated their opinions based on current data. On what else would you base it? For example, it's only natural for a truck driver who has driven the prairie roads for 30 years to feel at ease discussing Canadian weather patterns in January. He's seen them firsthand for decades. Felt them even, and risked his safety in their outcomes. Imagine that weather conditions have been milder over the latest few years, the driver may be inclined to believe that the upcoming trip through Regina, Saskatchewan, or Duluth, Minnesota, will be similar to last year's experiences, rather than reflecting long-term average conditions. He may even remember a specific drive through the region and the stops that he made along the way. These recollections will undoubtedly influence his behavior. He may even decide not to bother checking the weather reports, or worse, to be ill-prepared for more traditional freezing temperatures and poor driving conditions.

The prices of bonds, real estate, and other interest-sensitive investments increase when interest rates drop. They are inversely related to changes in interest levels. Real estate reacts to interest rates because most people have to borrow to buy it. When the cost of borrowing drops, high-priced real estate becomes more affordable, driving up prices of homes with the increased demand.

In the late 1970s, interest rates rose dramatically to fight the steeply rising cost of living. Both the US federal funds rate and the Bank of Canada rate peaked near 20% in 1982, and have been falling steadily ever since (Source: Bank of Canada and Federal Reserve). It wasn't until after this peak that bonds finally delivered a return in excess of the rate of inflation. Interest-sensitive investments perform best when interest rates fall.

Both bonds and real estate have provided returns far higher than their expected average long-run returns since the peak in interest rates in the early 1980s. Even more recently, real estate investors enjoyed unprecedented returns. In the spring of 2018, Vancouver's lower mainland real estate prices had increased by almost 85%, and in Metro Toronto by nearly 65% over the preceding five years.[3]

In 1988 and 2003, Karl Case and Robert Shiller, the scholars behind the Case-Shiller real estate index benchmark, studied the US price appreciation events at that time. In their surveys, people in major US centers felt that real estate prices would increase over the long-term. The communities, including Los Angeles, San Francisco, Boston, and Milwaukee, expected real estate prices to increase by 11.7% to 15.7% per year for the next 10 years.[4] At 11.7%, the value of a home will triple over ten years. Such expectations aligned with their recent experiences. Availability bias and the recency effect lead you to expect the past to repeat itself rather than revert to long-run trends. However, it is important to note that real estate gains have not always been so dramatic. While prevailing conditions can last for long periods, trends typically revert to the much longer overarching averages. Over the last 100 years, US housing and land has only risen by a half of a percent over the rate of inflation.[5]

Social changes and technological advancements are structural influences on long-term economic trends. The 2020 pandemic, for example, unexpectedly revised the economy by forcing businesses and employees to implement video conferencing and remote workplace logins. These behavioral changes, which were permanently adopted, altered commercial real estate use thereafter.

One of the most pervasive transformations of real estate use is on the horizon and in view. Over the coming years, autonomous electric cars and the impending revolution of Transportation as a Service (TaaS) will irreversibly alter both residential and commercial real estate uses.

As electric vehicle infrastructure continues to grow and autonomous driving technology becomes widely adopted, driverless ride-sharing will render single family cars a luxury rather than necessity. Instead of buying, insuring, maintaining, fueling, and parking a depreciating asset, a more affordable subscription service will make this option so compelling that individually owned vehicles will become less necessary, especially in urban centers. The impact of TaaS will provide families with thousands of dollars in savings every year.

In turn, consider how such a disruption will affect real estate. For example, parking garages in prime locations will be little used and the garage in your home can be converted to additional living space. Individuals can commute more easily, too, making the decision to live near work less important.

Between increased work-from-home options and the impending impact of autonomous electric vehicles, real estate use will be inevitably diverted from major cities to a wider diaspora. TaaS will be the biggest technologically disruptive shift in our economic landscape in the foreseeable future.

Real estate is generally considered a long-term asset because a homeowner usually remains in their property for many years. It also requires a proportionately large sum of capital to buy, and real estate transactions are relatively complex. When property demand is high and transactions turn over quickly, it is easy to forget that real estate isn't always easy to sell. When market prices drop, it can take much more time and effort to liquidate high-priced assets.

Also, when real estate prices are falling, there are few buyers, and it becomes illiquid. When real estate prices drop, holders tend to wait out a depression in transaction prices. That is part of the reason why a housing shortage developed after the 2008 financial crisis. Those who owned bare land didn't want to sell at reduced prices and developers didn't want to pay the pre-recession prices, leading to reduced residential home construction.

Case and Shiller also found that house prices are "sticky" during oversupply, while prices naturally fall in other kinds of markets. Not surprisingly, homeowners don't want to sell where they live if the price is low unless they have to for different reasons. Most people feel that they can wait it out, and listing a home during tough times is not common. Also, studies on **anchoring** and **loss aversion** demonstrate that people are unwilling to sell below the price they originally paid for a home, even if the price offered is fair in the current market.

There are natural exceptions to the rule. Consider a small resort town where building costs are high due to unpredictable snowfall and narrow, icy roads. Ski hills in Canada pose a myriad of obstacles for builders. Their work is complicated by a limited building season, transportation of building materials, limited access to trades, and steep building terrain. These areas have more volatile prices because a vacation property is a luxury. When people want to reduce or eliminate extra expenses during fiscal tightening, the ski chalet is on the auction block before the primary home.

The prices of real estate don't always rise, but they are significantly more resilient than other assets. During the Great Recession of 2008, the Canadian home price gauge slipped only a modest 5.47%, while the S&P/TSX® Canadian stock exchange index plunged −31% (Source: Refinitiv). This resiliency is partly because real estate is valued only once a year. Comparatively, stocks and ETFs post up-to-the-minute prices that engage our emotional reaction to loss aversion and **hindsight bias**. It's also beneficial that we have to live somewhere, insofar as we are less inclined to buy and sell real estate frequently. Suppose you had to pack up all of your belongings every time you traded assets in your retirement account.

Negative factors that should deflate real estate prices decrease liquidity instead. Real estate is more difficult to sell when prices soften. Risks to lower prices include such factors as a gap in immigration; changes in national regulations; permanent changes in the ability of workers to work from home; overbuilding; rising interest rates; and new tax-regimes such as the addition of speculation tax, empty-home taxes, and increased income taxes for short-term rentals. However, the single-most impactful disruption in real estate will be the progress of TaaS over the coming years, and the transformation of real estate in major cities.

The natural tendency to rely on strategies that have resulted in recent success makes adaptation to new conventions more difficult. Similar to the effects of anchoring, once we have a strategy in our toolbelt that has served us well, it's tough to let go of it. More often than not, you'll be more inclined to alter your view than to make a wholesale change based on new information. In the case of real estate, being unable to completely relinquish the belief that real estate only appreciates may unexpectedly increase your exposure to illiquidity.

The risk of real estate dropping dramatically is lower than for easily traded securities, such as stocks or bonds. Nevertheless, investors will face a deterioration in liquidity when disruption to the real estate market inevitably occurs. To guard against this risk, ensure that your leverage is manageable under a variety of situations, especially rising interest rates. An unexpected or relatively high increase in rates, compared to current rates near zero, are the same factors that can instigate the illiquidity in the first place. If you can't afford your mortgage, and you can't find a buyer, you'll be forced into a situation that will pose a significant financial burden.

Coupled with confirmation bias (the tendency to look for data to support what you already believe), the recency effect and availability bias hinder your objectivity. You rely on what you recall easily and will likely disregard new or unexpected information that doesn't fit your assumptions. These biases hinder your ability to identify unexpected risks.

To limit the influence of recency effect and availability bias, it's helpful to incorporate long-term trends into your forecasts. This step provides better insights about whether current market conditions are at extreme levels, and how your outlook may be skewed.

SUNK COST: Why Camping Seems Affordable

after you spend cash
and you can't get a refund
you are committed

You've likely heard about **sunk costs** before. You can't get back money already spent, so instead you want to get your money's worth. If there is an hour and a half wait to dine at your favorite restaurant, you may decide to leave. If you've already stood in line for an hour when you find out that there will be another half-hour wait, you're more likely to stay because of the time already invested.

Disneyland's ride wait lines effectively take advantage of our **sunk-cost bias.** By deceptively hiding parts of the line-up – looping inside and outside of buildings – ride-goers don't see how long the line is until they've spent too much time to then abandon the queue. Camping is another of life's adventures that plays into this bias by leading you to believe that it is an affordable holiday.

As far as vacations go, camping is considered a low-cost adventure, widely appealing because of its affordability. There are plenty of inexpensive or free sites across North and South America to set up your one-of-a-kind experience, but beware of the holiday that claims to be free, but instead plays into your sunk-cost bias.

According to the annual Kampgrounds of America's (KOA) North American Camping Report, a growing number of campers say that they want to camp more. The popularity of camping has been increasing, while the costs of flights, hotels, and restaurants stretch beyond the reach of young couples and families.[6]

Like wildfire sweeping across the forests of California and British Columbia, it's the millennials and Gen Z behind the popularity, and this is shaping the new era of camping. The under-40 crowd places such a high importance on getting outdoors that stand-up paddleboarding is a *thing*.

There's an appealing simplicity to propping up a nylon tent with a few aluminum poles and throwing down a thermal zippered sleeping bag. There's an art to finding and arranging granite stones in a circle, and knowing which dry, fallen branches are suitable for tinder. Experience with tripods, matches, and tent-pegs brings people together for a common purpose.

In comparison, a holiday flanked by 45-minute security lines, last-minute gate changes, and attempts to shove a 24-inch-diameter blue duffle bag into an 18-inch overhead bin without crushing its contents isn't necessarily stress-reducing. Filling your lungs with crisp air and bathing with a bar of Ivory in a glacier-fed lake can bring your senses alive in a way that the stale, recycled air from a hotel's HVAC system cannot.

Reconnecting with nature provides grounding not found in the sterility of a bustling hotel lobby, littered with suitcases and brightly lit shop windows. If the cost of a plane ticket to the Golden Temple of Dambulla was the same price as pitching a tent, free-spirited campers would pass up smoky morning-hair and tinfoil dinners for the Eiffel Tower and endless lattes along the River Seine. Watching credit card debt from a trip abroad ravage your savings account all at once is much more painful than buying a few items at a time. Adding to a camp-collection in the wooden-slat storage room one piece at a time is a more leisurely pace of spending.

The opportunity to be out in the wild is worth the cost of giving up cellular data coverage, according to the Kampgrounds' most recent report. A shockingly high 71% of the people who grew up not knowing a time before the internet are willing to give up their beloved technology to escape into nature.

The allure isn't only the camping, per se. Selecting the perfect remote location, organizing the gear into labeled plastic containers with snap-on lids, is as enjoyable as relishing the research time to accumulate the amenities. There's immense pleasure in discovering the ingenious gadgetry that hallmarks a holiday of roughing it.

"Camping is an activity that elicits excitement and pleasure even before the trip takes place. Almost two-thirds of campers find trip planning to be at least somewhat pleasant, which is well above the other types of planning for purchases," according to the report. By planning, we mean making lists and spending money, not all at once, but a little at a time: a sale-priced item here, a discounted outdoor convenience there.

Toss a frog into boiling water and it will leap back out immediately. Legend has it, however, that if you put that same frog into cold water and slowly bring it to a boil, the frog will stay put until it is firmly cooked. A slow spending pace has a similar effect. A flashlight costs only a few dollars. Buying affordable vacation ingredients one at a time is more palatable than putting money away for a trip that you're hoping for but can't afford yet. There is something satisfying about buying additional pieces of a collection.

Camping-gear Checklist:

16' × 9' extended dome tent

Extra tarp or canopy

Tent repair kit

Portable propane stove with collapsible stand, matches/lighter, and propane

Tablecloth

12-pack fire-starter sticks

Folding shovel with high carbon steel handle and nylon carry case

Coleman 5-Gallon Solar Shower

Tick remover, insect repellant, and SPF 30

First-aid kit

Collapsible 10-liter water basin

Paring knife, spatula, cooking spoon

Biodegradable soap, sponge, dishcloth, dishtowel

Coleman instant canopy sun wall

Ultra-light, portable 3-season sleeping bag

Ultimate backpack chair with cooler

Portable 5-gallon folding water storage container

Roasting sticks

Food storage containers and egg carrier

Multi-spice dispenser

9-cup aluminum coffee percolator

20-pack puncture-proof large trash bags

1600 lumen ultra-bright L.E.D. flashlight with four light modes and adjustable focus for emergency

Plates, bowls, cups, utensils

Cutting board

Paper towels

Puncture-proof folding ground cover

Inflatable foam camp pillow

Flashlights or headlamps, lantern, and batteries

3-in-1 pot set

2-pack camping lantern L.E.D. camp light

Camp stove toaster

25-foot 3/16-inch clothesline and wooden clothespins

4-in-1 portable stainless-steel camping utensil

Portable cooler with wheels

Multipurpose outdoor survival tools

Pop-up mesh umbrella food covers

A 25-foot roll of tin foil

Rainwear, gloves, hats, & hiking shoes

Maps, bikes, toys, etc.

Acquiring a new camping contraption is as pleasant as imagining the enjoyment you'll get from its use, and how each item will improve the overall experience. Every time another comfort is added, the perceived enjoyment utility increases until you have more stuff than you can carry. Have you ever met a camper who doesn't dream of getting a thing that can do something meaningful that only needs to be done because the camper has left the comforts of home?

Long forgotten is the R.V. financing, Sunday mornings perusing the aisles of Walmart, and Amazon searches scoping out the gear that will improve your experience under the stars. Of course, you can use those items more than once, so it's an investment, a sunk cost, an "in-for-a-penny, in-for-a-pound" type of false economy. Once the money is gone and the goods are piled up in the garage, it only makes sense to keep camping. Camping is not expensive, once you've acquired all the stuff you need to camp.

Mountain Equipment Co-Op was born in 1971 by six mountaineers in Vancouver, their website says. There were limited sources for mountaineering, ski mountaineering, hiking, and rock-climbing supplies. The band opened a cooperative among investors to provide gear locally with a little markup on the wholesale prices.

Today, the company charges relatively similar prices compared to other retail outlets. It has rebranded itself as M.E.C., a more contemporary name. It was still a co-op under the Canada Revenue Agency (CRA), until it was bought out during the challenging economy of the pandemic in 2020. Formerly, the co-op boasted that lifetime membership has never increased from the original $5, which for the early adopters was more in line with an investment of almost $50 today, given inflation since 1971.[7]

M.E.C. maintains a niche that appeals both to the tax laws and its prime consumer base. The value of five dollars has dropped simply due to inflation. Five bucks doesn't buy what it used to, yet it keeps members loyal. Handing over $50 for membership would scare some purchasers away. Five dollars garners marginal loyalty. It's low enough to consider becoming a member even for a single purchase. It might not prevent you from buying at another store, but there's still an affiliation that we connect to once we pay the fee.

The contingent nature of buying from M.E.C. to receive your dividends is captivating. To be eligible for any distribution, a large purchase during the year, or having patronage shares, sounds like the best tactic. You must invest in the business to benefit. So, we do. It's nice to feel like we belong.

Amazon figured that out, too, and uses its Prime membership to keep us coming back for camping gear and a wide variety of other widely available items from its sellers. The doorstep delivery system is convenient, too. The benefits of signing up for a Prime membership are of value enough to be enticing. Once you've invested in the annual payment, you're more likely to use the online retailer for repeat purchases. You might as well, since you've paid for it already.

When we make an initial investment of money, time, or emotion, it's more challenging to walk away from what we have already spent. It isn't easy to leave something of value unspent and unused, even when it's a token amount. It's easier to justify using it as some demonstration of frugality. However, it likely involves spending more money or more time. It's easier to take the next step, wait a bit longer, or invest a bit more to see it through than to forget about it altogether, even when the sunk cost is small.

Is camping an affordable holiday, or is it partly just the way we think about spending? We can justify small expenditures, even when they add up over time to large amounts. Spending on pieces is more comfortable than staring at one significant invoice. A luxury holiday, one piece at a time, drives a less emotional reaction than paying a large sum. Buying a little something is more fun than saving a little for something less real in the future.

Perhaps camping is so compelling because we already have the gear; however, small costs over long periods can add up without being noticed, but if these sunk costs compel you to improve your life by getting outdoors more often, then use it to your advantage. Also, a season's pass to the ski hill usually results in more days enjoying the mountainside compared to someone who only pays for one day-pass at a time.

The same theory applies to buying cheaper inferior goods that may need repairs or replacement more often than the more costly version of better quality. Regardless of what you sink your money into, you will feel a greater sense of obligation to use it. In any event, ensure that you aren't settling for the seemingly affordable option, when in fact, it may be just as expensive over the long run as something else you prefer.

BARNUM AND FORER EFFECT: A Fool Is Born Every Minute

economists who recommend a cautious stance may be right or wrong

The Ringling Brothers & Barnum & Bailey circus was billed as the "Greatest Show on Earth." From an early age, Phineas Taylor (P.T.) Barnum learned that human behavior was biased, and reliable enough to exploit for profit. "I don't believe in duping the public," he asserted, "I believe in first attracting and then pleasing them."[8]

Barnum ventured into a wide variety of businesses. He operated a free-spirited newspaper for which his opinions resulted in charges of libel. His Connecticut State lottery ran successfully until lotteries became illegal. He gambled on real estate speculation and created a book auction and several other entrepreneurial, unique, and profitable pursuits. By his mid-twenties, Barnum's business interests turned to showmanship when he purchased Scudder's American Theatre. He hung a lighthouse lamp at the front of the building to draw the attention of everyone in range, spoiling the dark streets of the mid-1800s New York City. By day, flags protruded from the top of the building, and garish, over-sized animal paintings hung in the windows. If the building adornments weren't enough to attract attention, the hot-air balloon rides lifting off the rooftop were.

The wooden structure at Broadway and Ann Street was the unlikely home to exotic animals, spectacles, and human rarities never seen before. This theater, which he named after himself, was no institutional gallery intended to maintain and display critical historical artifacts. Barnum curated a selection of freaks and hoaxes crafted to dupe consumers, predating twentieth-century reality TV by 100 years.

He "leased" a blind and almost paralyzed slave woman named Joice Heth, and would have bought her if New York hadn't outlawed slavery by that time. He exhibited her for 10–12 hours a day with claims that not only was she 161 years old, but was also the former nurse of George Washington. Shortly after that, she died (at no more than 80 years of age), and Barnum phlegmatically sold tickets to view her autopsy for 50 cents apiece to curious spectators.

In 1842, Barnum also purchased the Fiji Mermaid for the exhibition: a taxidermy primate body sewn onto the bottom half of a fish. The success of each curiosity brought on the next bigger, better, or stranger display. The "smallest person that ever walked alone" was one of the most notorious spectacles. The four-year-old General Tom Thumb was called an adult dwarf. To enhance the performance, he was taught to imitate prominent figures like Hercules and Napoleon. By the time he was five, he was drinking wine and smoking cigars.[9]

For Barnum, the illusion wasn't as beguiling as the business of who can be fooled by it. He maintained that the theatrics were only intended to attract and entertain his audiences. He remained unconcerned, however, with the level of fiction required for success, famously recounting, "There's a sucker born every minute."

It wasn't until the later part of his life that Barnum established the P. T. Barnum's Grand Traveling Museum, Menagerie, Caravan, & Hippodrome. He purchased a train to move the tents, animals, and performers from location to location in his traveling three-ring circus. He collaborated with Bailey and others, ultimately selling his interest. By 1970, the famous carnival that had tricked audiences for over 145 years had closed its tent doors.

Barnum's notorious history of deceiving viewers with near-truths has won him a place in history. An ambiguous narrative that can apply to a wide variety of people or situations is referred to as both the **Barnum effect** and the **Forer effect,** interchangeably. By using detailed words and phrases that can apply to a multitude of examples, we tend to feel that they are accurate and informative. Yet, on closer examination, you can often see the ambiguity and generalizations that are not as specific as you first thought.

Horoscopes are a good example of the Forer or Barnum effect. Since the description of each zodiac sign is distinctly different from the next, it's easier to buy into the advice that follows because it seems to be specific to you. People are willing to give false-legitimacy to fortune telling, especially when some of the advice sounds plausible and relatable to our circumstances, or when we want it to be true. Both *wishful thinking* and confirmation bias contribute to the impression. Yet, with wider reflection, you may also see that the details are more general than you may have initially thought. You will tend to feel that the writer has some personal insight to your character when they could not possibly know you at all, which supports the idea that horoscopes are omniscient, or all-knowing.

This outcome isn't limited to describing personalities or predicting your future love entanglements. We are subject to overestimating the precision of such nebulous accounts on any topics. Economic and investment prognosticators have learned the lessons of soothsayers and palm readers, and regularly offer the same types of vague advice. Whether intentional or not, statements such as "the geopolitical risks have heightened" and "be wary of the lofty price-to-earnings multiples" are hard to disagree with, regardless of current market conditions. These types of recommendations are obscure enough to be true in any economic climate, and despite the seemingly important message are useless. When you re-read the statement critically, you can see that the advice is so imprecise that it has no practical value.

The agreeability is what sticks with you. You will tend to remember points that support your existing economic outlook: confirmation bias at work again. Frankly, people want to be right. People make up their minds that they are right and look for corroborating evidence to support their views.

It is foolhardy to give meaning to vague messages, yet you will be tempted to align these types of messages with your existing opinions. Broad statements can be deceivingly accommodative at first glance, when, they provide no useful information at all.

Read economic projections and general recommendations with a critical eye. Identify actionable instruction, if any, and discard nonspecific opinions. When recommendations – such as to be cautious – can be applied too widely or are equally effective in opposing scenarios, the advice is not as helpful or predictive as it may first appear.

LOSS AVERSION UNDERMINES YOUR BELIEFS:
Trading Money for Sleep

*selling your holdings
to avoid the discomfort
won't produce returns*

Pundits had begun publishing opinions in the latter part of the summer of 2018, predicting the end of the bull market. They were prognosticating the next recession with such frequency that investment professionals and consumers alike began wondering if the outcome was inevitable. The growing sentiment developed into trigger-happy index fingers hovering over the sell button, ready to depress it at the slightest evidence of a downdraft. By November that year, speculation morphed into a wave of consensus. The longest-running economic expansion was long overdue to retreat.

The narrative was that past economic cycles hadn't lasted much longer than this one had already run and this one was simply past due. The expansion that had begun in March 2009 was *long in the tooth*, some said.

Capital market prices rise because there are more buyers than sellers. All it takes is a quantitative shift in the general sentiment to change its direction. Investors are people, each of whom is endowed with bias. Sometimes, fundamental reasons for a change in market direction may be unclear. In every case, however, a change in the market trend is due to consensus of the investment public.

Leading up to the stock market decline that year, investors had been optimistic about continued growth. North American unemployment had dropped comfortably to the lowest levels seen in multiple decades. In both Canada and the US, most people who wanted to work were able to find a job. Sentiment is just as important in market conditions as fundamental evidence when people are making investment decisions.

Besides, the almighty consumer was spending like their wallet had been dunked in the fountain of youth, with substantially higher Black Friday sales than in any other year in history. Business and earnings continued expanding, pushing up both house values and stock prices in lockstep. The anticipated recession was seemingly not imminent, the pundits claimed. Yet, with a cocked eyebrow, they cautioned that it was lurking. The prediction was specific enough to cause alarm but vague enough to be as useful as reading your horoscope – the Barnum effect.

Without the benefit of clairvoyance, a cautious approach is wise. However, the insidious nature of widespread alarm is that the rising levels of caution can initiate the cascade of what is feared. It's a self-fulfilling prophecy.

The stock market indexes across North America dropped 20% between September and December 2018 (Source: Refinitiv). The smackdown broadly hit every sector without discretion. No dividend-paying shares, value stocks, promising technology companies, or new-economy disruptors were able to maintain their share prices.

During extreme events, when investors sell everything to raise cash, diversification isn't very helpful. When liquidity dries up, every type of security declines in concert, regardless of the type, sector, class, or any other qualities. In this case, investors capitulated, throwing out the proverbial baby with the bathwater. The prospect of a recession may have instigated some investors to sell. Others sold for fear of the dropping values, while some liquidated because they had a predefined exit strategy triggered by the initial drop.

Eventually, margin calls forced leveraged investors to cash-out to cover their investment loans. Each investor who sold their holdings as the market plummeted thought of reasons to justify the trade. The motives to sell during a market capitulation are rarely rooted in a long-term plan. If they were, the market would never be oversold.

The last of the beleaguered investors that couldn't feel a bottom to the market drop, made one. Those who couldn't stomach the volatility any longer finally dumped their positions on Christmas Eve. Perhaps they thought it was prudent to eliminate the market-driven anxiety brought on by **loss aversion**. That way, they could relax over the holidays and focus on family gatherings, a glass of eggnog, and too much turkey stuffing instead. December 24th marked the last trading day to claim capital losses in that year, as well. It also marked the lowest price level of the S&P500® and S&P/TSX® before the price recovery began (Source: Refinitiv). It is uncanny how many people sell stocks on the final day of a meltdown. It is as if people reach an emotional capitulation simultaneously. Everyone who liquidates at the bottom of the market is quick to explain, ironically, that they decided to prevent further losses.

Selling securities during periods of extreme volatility avoids the negative emotional experiencing of loss aversion. By doing so, however, you run the risk of sustaining an unrecoverable loss. The moment when selling securities will cause the steepest financial damage seems to be the most emotionally compelling time to take such action. Yet, the compelling nature of loss aversion makes it easy to bluff yourself into thinking that you are acting prudently, in the name of relief and a good night's rest. Sleep promotes well-being, but giving up on a well-constructed investment strategy when markets become volatile is not in the best interest of anyone's financial health. However, by the end of this book, you'll have other ways to ensure a good night's sleep, instead of trading your money for it.

HERD MENTALITY: Consensus Hurts Performance

if you're last to buy
the easy money is gone
and risks are higher

In the mid-century, it was common for North American families to gather around the television with foldout TV trays and Swanson TV dinners. The metal, partitioned plate containing Salisbury steak, mashed potatoes, peas with butter, and peach cobbler was considered a treat. The popular weekly ritual often included the whole family watching Walt Disney documentary programming.

In 1958, *White Wilderness, Part II, The Lemmings and Arctic Bird Life* aired, notoriously depicting a dramatic scene of small, furry rodents trundling about the arctic tundra. They followed each other down a steep embankment and ultimately over the edge of a cliff as they "committed mass suicide by rushing into the sea in droves."

The playful background music and unemotional male voice-over describe the harrowing tale of these seemingly mindless, lovable creatures. "Their frenzy takes them tumbling down the terraced cliffs creating tiny avalanches of sliding soil and rocks," the voice narrates. Then, the oboes and bassoons register a dramatic shift in tone as the undeterred lemmings push forward to the precipice of the final cliff. "This is the last chance to turn back," the speaker cautions the frozen audience gripping a forkful of margarine-flavored mashed potatoes. "Yet over they go."

Lemming after lemming leaps over the edge of the cliff, splatting onto the surface of the Arctic Sea like bath toys tossed into the tub. Even then, they didn't turn back toward the shore. Collectively, they swim away from the safety of the beach, into the consuming cold waves. "Gradually strength wanes," he continues as blandly as if describing the color of olive-green draperies, "determination ebbs away, and soon the Arctic Sea is dotted with tiny bobbing bodies."

The drama of the lemmings' **herd mentality** has gone from folklore to well-regarded axiom. Urban legend speculates that the producers bought the lemmings and pushed them off the cliff to produce their show. Whether that's true or not, the 1958 movie sequence isn't a common example of lemmings' natural migration behavior.

Perhaps it was the drama of it all, and the vast viewership that Disney commanded at that time. Whatever the reason, the story of the lemmings stuck, and is used as a reference today when describing the behavior of investors during asset price bubbles and their ultimate crashes.

There is strength in numbers, and following the crowd leaves you with the sense that you're on the right track. After all, everyone else is doing it. It is more challenging to act out of sync with the rest of the world. You're left with nagging doubt about your choices when you're the only one going in a different direction.

When it comes to investing, however, consensus hurts performance. Doing what other investors are doing works against you. Mathematically, as more investors buy or sell a particular strategy, your risks increase and your opportunity for returns diminishes.

Nevertheless, there is ample evidence among institutional and individual investors that herd mentality is alive and well. People still tend to make investment decisions in a coordinated fashion. For example, when a stock performs well for long periods, investors are more inclined to continue to buy its shares. As the price rises, we seem to feel validated that we made a profitable investment (confirmation bias). Then, when other investors participate, we have the added pleasure of being part of a crowd of profitable investors. Validation feeds our desire to be right. There are many examples illustrating the power of herd mentality and confirmation bias in motivating investors to buy or sell, regardless of the merits of the investment.

When investors are net buyers of a specific rising stock this month, it's more likely that they will be buyers of that company again next month, unless the share price declines. Investors also have the odd proclivity to buy fewer stocks than they sell, tending to consolidate holdings. This pattern implies a preference for popular stocks, and a concentration of them. There is further evidence that we prefer to buy shares with an unusually high trading volume. These all point to our tendency to fall in line with what other investors do.[10]

Reflecting on your past investing behavior, you may now recognize how often you feel compelled to act due to a price change or because you see other investors jumping in or leaving a strategy. It is tempting to rely on the decisions of others rather than taking the time to investigate your options. Without analysis, however, trading decisions are influenced by herd mentality or other behavioral dispositions such as anchoring, overconfidence, confirmation bias, disposition effect, availability bias, and representativeness.

Yet, there are risks to being part of the crowd of investors. Assume that the incoming US president is against carbon-based energy. In that scenario, you decide to sell your pipelines and oil companies and buy renewable energy stocks. That may be a good strategy. However, if you generated such reasoning, others will likely have thought of it as well. By the time news of the president's platform is announced, it's safe to assume that the impact of the announcement will already be priced into the value of stocks. If that's true, the upside gains you'd expect are already taken.

Moreover, when you hear about a stock because it is up 300%, you may feel the urge to buy shares so that you don't miss out on the rest of the increase. The rise in price, however, isn't evidence that it's a good investment or that its suitable for your strategy. It may not even be a profitable business. Your natural tendency to follow the crowd leaves later investors with less potential profit at a higher risk. Early adopters – notably *not* the herd followers – profit the most from any investment strategy.

As an example, consider the merits of Netflix, Inc. (NFLX). It is a company familiar to thousands of households in North America and other nations. The low monthly subscription price and accessible format are why millions of subscribers binge-watch whole seasons of *Bridgerton* and *Grey's Anatomy* over a weekend.

NFLX transformed from a household entertainment provider to a stock market darling during an era of communications business disruption. Recall that you will tend to be more comfortable investing in shares of companies that you know and understand, especially when you are reminded of their products and services daily. **Familiarity bias** leads you to feel that the investment has lower risk than unfamiliar alternatives. In reality, there is a meaningful preference to choose what is comfortable or even fashionable. Herd mentality similarly prompts you to expect higher returns due to the strategy's popularity.

In the case of NFLX, many investors and analysts did their homework early on, and bought or recommended the shares. Companies that interrupt the **status quo** and force old businesses to adapt to more effective business processes also beguile investors with a promise for high, or even excessive, earnings growth. Yet, a wide number of consumers who recognized that the service was gaining marketplace traction quickly, bought shares on a hunch.

When veneer-cabinet television sets first entered living rooms in the 1950s, programmers monetized the popular shows with product placements. Crinoline-skirted women would oddly break from the scene and peer straight into the camera to lift a box of detergent, extolling its effectiveness over all other brands. Product placement morphed into commercial breaks that TV watchers, unwilling to cross the room to turn the dial, accepted as a necessary evil. Then, viewers were able to channel surf during commercial breaks, to the frustration of whomever was not in control of the remote control, and eventually, they could skip advertisements altogether by recording their favorite programs on a personal video recorder (PVR). That's where streaming services came in and changed everything, again. Airing advertising content wasn't profitable any more, when consumers no longer had to watch the commercials. To remain competitive, new media companies needed to offer the best content on demand to entice subscribers to pay for their service.

The Netflix service swept North America and other nations. They acquired access to top-rated movies and miniseries, and ultimately began developing and airing proprietary shows. It was a compelling offer at a relatively low monthly fee compared to the pre-programming satellite services that predated this evolution. This new approach gutted the customer base of the old format cable and satellite channels that only offered fixed showtimes and annoying commercial interruptions.

It didn't take content providers like Disney long to realize that instead of renting out their beloved animated movies and iconic series, they could set up their own streaming-service, eliminating the middleman. They developed a proprietary platform to deliver their award-winning shows, circumventing NFLX and other streaming services.

Despite competition, NFLX has enjoyed steady subscription growth since 1997, and with it, stellar earnings. The company's success delighted investors with a rising stock price. The profits hailed increasing enthusiasm by a fresh set of investors, cheering the stock price ever higher. Fact-checking and analysis is diminished in importance, replaced by natural bias mechanisms for making decisions quickly, with mistaken efficiency. The rising stock price and profits feel like validation of your choice to invest and remain invested. Confirmation bias and herd mentality tend to take over the helm when you're profiting.

At the tipping point, investors begin to realize that parabolic earnings growth isn't sustainable. Share prices eventually reflect a slowing growth rate. Share prices can't climb beyond earnings indefinitely. Moreover, for NFLX, there are a finite number of people who can subscribe to the service. The more customers you have, the fewer new subscriptions you can add.

Enthusiasm for NFLX pushed the shares to 300 times reported earnings of $1.43, by the third quarter of 2017. Investment analysts predicted future earnings growth at a delightfully stunning rate of 88% to $2.69 for the full year in 2018 (Source: Refinitiv). It's no wonder that investors were giddy, lining up to buy more shares even at such an inflated price. However, the company would have to continue at that pace of growth without faltering for the next six years to justify today's price-tag. That is to say that in 2017, NFLX was trading at 2023's intrinsic value if the company were able to sustain 88% growth.

Herd mentality is typical among both institutional and individual investors, but for different reasons. Consider the story of Tulpaenmanie.

The famous Viennese biologist Carolus Clusius first introduced the cultivated tulip bulb for which the Netherlands is now renowned. When launched in the late 1500s, the cultivated bulbs offered unique properties that spiked their popularity. Traders sought the exceptional flowers for medicinal purposes as often as for adorning gardens. Ultimately, the bulbs established a functional status as a product of trade.

As interest grew, the number of hybrid species multiplied, further enhancing their appeal and demand, driving prices even higher. Eventually, not wanting to be left out of professional traders' profits, the enthusiasm for tulip bulbs spread among commoners willing to sell other assets to participate in the frenzy.

A few hundred years after the tulip bubble, John Maynard Keynes, the British economist responsible for influencing how governments manage their economies, warned other investors with sage advice. "The market can be irrational longer than you can remain solvent." Don't be hasty to anticipate a profit too quickly.

The delusion of herd mentality and collective public opinion can persist for a long time. You may be correct in your investment research, but if the rest of the market doesn't follow suit, you may appear to have made a wrong choice for a painfully long and unprofitable time. Delusional trading during Tulpaenmanie lasted more than three decades. By February 1637, traders reportedly paid more than 10 times a craftsman's annual income for a single bulb.[11] If you had shorted the tulip market in the early 1600s, you might well have bankrupted yourself.

In 2020, as the worldwide Covid-19 pandemic exploded and companies scrambled to adopt remote business technologies, investors were scrambling, too. The company Zoom Technologies Inc. (ZTNO) rose from $1.10 on January 1 to $20.90 on March 20, 2020. On November 12, just a few months later, it closed at 16 cents. Those investors likely thought they were investing in Zoom Video Communications Inc. (ZM), which traded on the Nasdaq. The video conferencing platform that became notoriously popular as businesspeople turned to virtual meetings, began the year at $62 and increased to $428.64 over the same time frame (Source: Refinitiv). Investors in ZTNO relied on **representativeness** by assuming that the misleading company name coupled with the noticeable price appreciation meant that they were invested in the right company. If they had the wrong stock entirely, they obviously replaced research with herd mentality and confirmation bias to buy and hold stock in the wrong company.

The stories of Tulpaenmanie, NFLX, and ZTNO all share the same underlying natural bias. Even so, some participants profited from the trades. Others rode the prices all the way up and all the way back down again. And still others lost their shirts. Nevertheless, in every case of frenzied investing and herd mentality, investors who participate later in the cycle operate at an elevated and sometimes unnecessary risk level.

Chapter 4

Developing Your Personal Economic Values

Why Commit to the Eight Steps?

The first three chapters illustrated many examples of seemingly rational thought processes that unwittingly derail your intentions and objectives. Thinking shortcuts lead to biases that can have serious consequences on your financial health. They also tend to cause unnecessary stress along the way. For example, you've seen how recent events have a greater impact on your risk appetite. What has happened most recently influences your future decisions more than you may have realized. Other tendencies, such as your natural inclination to treat one pile of money differently from another or justify your actions by altering your beliefs, undermines your goals rather than helps you reach them.

When current market trends are enticing or your neighbor's success is beguiling, it is easy to lose focus of the objectives that are most important to you. During periods of volatility, when the genuine fear of loss is unnerving, you may find yourself grasping at straws and making haphazard decisions that don't lead you to where you want to go.

Despite the influence of natural bias, however, you can retain control of your economic ambitions. The best way to achieve your goals and limit the effects of judgment errors is first to understand what you value and why these are important to you.

By investing time now to establish your values and implement habits to limit the impact of bias, you can achieve your goals and objectives with less effort and grief by avoiding many of the errors of transactional decisions. You can meaningfully reduce the emotional stress of urgent situations by applying simple yet effective habits to the financial choices you make. And, as the benefits of adopting these habits evolves, your increased success will become self-motivating. Of all the habits that are introduced over the coming chapters, the most critical is to understand your **personal economic values (PEVs)**.

Although some investors have found success in adopting certain axioms to thwart destructive tendencies, applying such broad advice can sometimes make matters worse. Nevertheless, these prophetic sayings would not be passed from teacher to student, parent to child, or become memes dotting the internet if not for certain recognizable truths within them.

They persist because decision-making errors are common among all of us. Most of this sage advice was crafted long before researchers began deciphering the systematic judgment errors and bias in decision-making. However, they have ended up in our vocabulary without instructions on how and when to apply them.

> *Buy low, sell high.* Proverb
> *It's not a loss until you sell.* Anonymous
> *Bulls make money. Bears make money. Pigs get slaughtered.* Jim Cramer's #1 rule
> *In investing, what is comfortable is rarely profitable.* Robert Arnott
> *A bird in the hand is worth two in the bush.* Proverb
> *Beware of little expenses; a small leak will sink a great ship.* Benjamin Franklin
> *I will tell you the secret to getting rich on Wall Street. You try to be greedy when others are fearful, and you try to be fearful when others are greedy.* Warren Buffett
> *The four most dangerous words in investing are: "This time it's different."* Sir John Templeton
> *Buy when everyone else is selling and hold until everyone else is buying.* J Paul Getty
> *The stock market is filled with individuals who know the price of everything but the value of nothing.* Philip Fisher

Axioms may help avoid some pitfalls, but when they are applied too broadly, following their advice can be downright dangerous. As emotions and biases kick in, trusting vague instructions – as you discovered with the **Barnum effect** – is as useful as following your weekly horoscope for guidance on choosing your ideal marriage partner. One or more of these sayings may have prevented you from selling all your investments at the bottom of the market cycle two years ago, but next time it may not be enough to deflect your naturally tendencies to capitulate thinking that you're avoiding risk.

Rules of thumb may also seem to be a reasonable approach to complex decisions. When facts are limited or time is constrained, drawing on earlier experiences sounds judicious. However, pre-programmed conclusions are often a poor proxy for the situation at hand. **Representativeness** leads you to assume that current conditions are more similar to the past than they really are. Substituting what you learned about another scenario may not translate as well as you think, and current realities may be too complicated to draw a valid conclusion from past experiences. Reflecting on rules of thumb is not always harmful. However, relying on them too heavily introduces **confirmation bias**, **overconfidence**, and a host of other biases to sway your choice.

Also, rules of thumb become less and less useful as the complexity of the situation increases. For example, someone might believe that exchanging Canadian for US dollars whenever oil drops is a reliable investment strategy. Sure, the strategy may reflect the general trend in which the mid-term price of West Texas Intermediate (WTI) crude oil moves in opposition to the value of US versus Canadian currency. Still, it doesn't mean you should put that trade decision on automatic pilot. Many other factors affect the foreign exchange markets, and it is foolhardy to rely on singular factors to predict outcomes regardless of the strength of the signal.

Economists discuss people's motivations as if we always act in our best interest and squeeze out maximum benefit at every turn. When in fact, people systematically demonstrate irrational financial conclusions that can erode wealth. Recall how fear generated by **loss aversion** creeps in when the capital markets become volatile. The **status quo bias** keeps you from deciding when your choices are too complicated, or when you are unclear about how best to proceed. Moreover, the fear of missing out and **herd mentality** beg you to buy stocks before it's too late, even when share prices are lofty and the investment doesn't suit your long-term goals.

You've read how hope rises when facing an inevitable loss influencing you to accept unnecessary risk at a time when you would be wise to cut your losses instead. And **hindsight bias** leads you to think that you could have prevented the loss altogether when you obviously would have if you had the foresight.

The negative impact of biased reasoning on your financial results puts your goals farther from reach. You may be solving a short-term problem, but you're not improving your long-term plans by making such transactional decisions. Relying on what ironically feels natural – relying on your gut – often leads you to false assessments that create worry, stress, and regret.

Impulsive decisions get a bad rap for good reason. Knee-jerk reactions, almost by definition, are shortsighted. They might be an efficient mechanism for getting stuff done and solving short-term issues, but the bias behind them can lead to poor long-term outcomes.

It stands to reason that if you make fewer transactional decisions, you will make fewer errors. Reducing the number of times that you have to make quick decisions – or decisions of any kind – can therefore reduce the impact of making the wrong ones. The number of possible economic blunders that you face is plentiful. And, the less often you suffer stressful financial events, the more likely you'll be able to reach your financial goals, and the happier you'll generally feel.

You can't avoid bias altogether, but you can dramatically reduce its role in two important ways:

1. By applying the long-term objectives of your PEVs to reduce the overall number of decisions you make.
2. By implementing habits that can help you manage the influences of bias in your choices.

While quick methods of processing information can be useful, you will produce better results when you understand and apply your values instead of deferring to the type of reasoning generated by remorse, fear, overconfidence, and the like. Once you start focusing on these tenets, you will begin heading in the right direction more consistently.

A sum of money isn't as meaningful as a goal that you can envision. Owning your own home to raise a family is a values-based objective. Traveling the world because your mother was a missionary and you want to preserve the legacy of her work, is another. Even buying a status symbol can be values-based if it is meaningful to you, such as owning a home in a certain country because you want to reestablish the roots of your family or because you want to be closer to people you love.

Becoming rich isn't a goal. The desire to be a millionaire or billionaire isn't as actionable because it doesn't describe what that signifies to you or why it is essential. Saying that you want to be rich isn't as telling as describing what it would look and feel like in real life. A numeric quest doesn't engage your values as well; anyone can pick a number out of the air.

Wealth develops as you synchronize your actions with your PEVs. Objectives become achievements when they are rooted in your values. It's easier to commit time and resources to well-thought-out PEVs than to a meaningless, esoteric number. Your objectives must make practical sense in terms of how you live your life, and a values-based plan is the best opportunity for success because it aligns with who you are and what is important to you.

Personal Economic Values Workbook

You may be able to complete these questions in one sitting by answering with your first instinctual thoughts. You may prefer, however, to invest an afternoon or read through the questions first. Then, reflect on them for a couple of days before sitting down to develop your responses. Either way, it is ideal to set aside a period of time without distraction in order to provide meaningful insight into your core beliefs, whatever they may be. First, start off with the most obvious entry: What is today's date?

Date: _____

Step 1: The Launch Point

Begin by answering the following questions to evaluate your current financial situation. The questions below – and other resources – are available on the book's website at www.unbiasedinvestor.org.

Use your own words. Your answers can be as short or as long as you wish. These questions are designed to recall your experiences and viewpoints, so they will be top of mind in the subsequent steps. These questions will also help you identify areas where you feel confident, and uncover those that require more attention. The answers you provide will ultimately lead to the development of your PEVs.

I feel best about my finances when…
My first memory of money was when…
If I die, my financial affairs are…
The current state of my investments is…
The money I've borrowed is…
The professionals that I enjoy working with are…
The characters that I don't want to deal with are…
The one piece of advice that I could use right now is…
The actions/processes I can delegate are…
I should stop spending on…
I want to learn more about…
I am most proud of my…
What keeps me up at night is…

Step 2: How Do You See Yourself?

Use the following space to list what you want to have in your life. These can be assets, adventures, experiences, or a way of living. For example, you may want to achieve a master's degree, run a marathon, or build a business. Experiences may include hiking the Himalayas, having grandchildren, or winning an award. You may want to acquire a family vacation property, an art collection, or a 26-foot catamaran.

Identifying what you want to have in your life will promote thinking about your future and set the stage for the financial resources you'll need to execute these objectives. Your intentions and life-objectives will determine the actions to take in the activities to follow.

Over my lifetime, I would like to achieve:

1.
2.
3.
4.

The adventures and experiences that I would like to have:

1.
2.
3.
4.

Assets that I would like to acquire over my lifetime:

1.
2.
3.
4.

Step 3: What Are Your Financial Skills?

A skill is an ability in which you have developed knowledge, experience, or proficiency. Everyone has varying degrees of knowledge and experience in managing money. You may acquire skills from formal education or everyday life. For example, as a long-time union worker, you may have a good understanding of how your pension plan works.

List the skills that apply to managing the various aspects of your finances, in which you have a high comfort level. Possible skills include budgeting, investment decisions, haggling, shopping, saving, financial planning, portfolio management, tax strategies, investment analysis, debt reduction, tax filing, and negotiations. There is no limit to the number of skills you may include on your list. Focus on the most useful financial skills that you have rather than compiling an exhaustive list.

Estimate your degree of comfort executing each skill you identify by circling whether you are knowledgeable, experienced, or proficient.

The third step is to clarify how you apply each skill in your daily life. For example, you may list investment decision-making as one of your skills, and circle "experienced" and "knowledgeable." In the description, you might clarify that you are able to assess your risk tolerance and investment performance accurately but prefer to have an advisor manage the daily investment decisions. Others might state that they enjoy making their own investment decisions.

By identifying your strengths, you can determine which roles you are willing to manage directly and which areas you prefer to engage outside resources or support.

Skill #1: _____
Knowledgeable/Experienced/Proficient
Description:
Skill #2: _____
Knowledgeable/Experienced/Proficient
Description:
Skill #3: _____
Knowledgeable/Experienced/Proficient
Description:
Skill #4: _____
Knowledgeable/Experienced/Proficient
Description:

Step 4: What Are Your Beliefs about Money?

Values are relatively permanent beliefs about what is critical, worthy, or just. Opinions are an invisible force that can influence your actions. Determining what you value will help you execute choices consistent with what you stand for and what you want to achieve. Your interpretation of values may not be the same as someone else's, and you may desire certain values more than others.

In this step, provide at least one value from each category of financial, saving, spending, and investing values. Limit the number of values you list to no more than three, focusing on those that are of primary importance to you:

- Possible *financial* values include career, education, security, passive income, profit, trust, family, or balance.
- Possible *savings* values include consistency, regularity, maximization, passive income, blue-chip, conservative, or active.
- Possible *spending* values include generosity, frugality, leverage, worth, minimalism, essentialism, luxury, quality, name-brand, or discount.
- Possible *investing* values include accuracy, active, transparency, quality, tax-sensitivity, innovation, social-minded, hedging, diversification, momentum, value, growth, risk-free, inflation protection, environmentally sensitive, stable, or cost-sensitive.

Examples:

Values: Green living

Description: I believe that the essential factor in living life, running a business, and choosing an investment is the environmental impact that I'm making.

Values: Quality purchases

Description: I prefer to spend more on something that is made well and of higher quality, knowing that it will last longer.

Values: Conservative investing

Description: I am not a risk-taker and prefer to know that my savings will be there in the morning, even if that means that I only earn a small return.

Values:

Description:

Values:

Description:

Values:

Description:

Values:

Description:

Step 5: Risk: Understanding Your Thresholds Is Critical

Most people tend to accept a game of chance when the reward is roughly double the wager. Most people also appreciate the value of a gain about half as much as they regret the same quantity lost. We also know that your appetite for risk is affected by what has recently happened in your life. After a recent win, you may be influenced by the house money effect, or in the case of a loss, you may be inclined to increase your risk, especially when you believe that there's an opportunity to regain the loss. Refer to Chapter 2 and review the desire to control risk, the follies of relying on intuition, and how people can feel compelled to increase their risk at the wrong time.

People generally view themselves within a consistent risk-framework, and categorize themselves as low, medium, or high risk-takers. Understanding your general risk tolerance helps to determine the types of investments that are suitable, which then determines the expected level of variable returns you can anticipate. It is vital to consider the impact of loss aversion on your outlook, and to think about how your choices may be influenced by your experiences. Once you understand your comfort level, you can establish barriers to avoid biased decisions that do not reflect your PEVs.

For the purpose of this discussion, we use the term *risk* to describe variability and volatility, rather than permanent loss of capital. The measures below are intended to reflect typical long-run market fluctuations, rather than extreme events. These can provide general guidelines to assess your tolerance for volatility and variability. Circle the most relevant level from the five categories below. Then, provide any additional comments to describe your willingness to accept risk or your discomfort with risk in your own words.

0% volatility: I don't expect the value of my assets to increase. My primary goal is to know my money will be there when I need it.

0–5% volatility: I can better protect my purchasing power over the long run by having some variability, but I prefer that most of my investments are reasonably stable.

5–10% volatility: Balance is an ideal mix for me. I understand market-traded assets fluctuate, but that diversifying my holdings will limit volatility. Also, reinvesting recurring income produced by my investments and selecting higher-quality investments is expected to keep volatility lower than the broad investment market.

10–20% volatility: I want to earn as much or more than the broad stock market. I cannot tolerate mediocre returns, but I can't afford to throw caution to the wind, either.

20%+ volatility: I don't mind taking a chance if the wins are big. I don't have daily financial issues to worry about, so I can afford to take chances and I'm rarely rattled.

Comments:

Step 6: What Is Holding You Back?

Bias results from thinking shortcuts that you use in everyday choices. People also rely on rules of thumb in decision-making, based on past successes and mistakes that they vow never to repeat. Everyone is susceptible to inter-ference from bias that can undermine the intended financial outcome. You may notice that certain biases are more influential in your life than others. Identifying which behaviors interfere in your financial decisions most often can help you to focus on the most critical habits for you to adopt.

List the three or four decisions that come to mind, made in the heat of the moment, that you later regretted. Then, describe what led up to those choices and your decision process. For convenience, you may want to skim through the various biases in the first three chapters to refresh your memory of typical scenarios that can cause unintended financial out-comes. Lastly, consider which steps you can take or habits you can adopt to avoid those situations. After reading the next chapter on adopting unbiased habits, feel free to come back to this step and add any habits that address your most critical issues, and can be easily integrated into your plan.

Examples:
Bias: Overtrading/Loss Aversion
Description: I check my investments every morning, especially when markets are volatile. I feel anxious when asset values drop and try to reduce my risk by selling when that happens.
Habit to adopt: I will keep a written log of my decisions, describing my rationale and how long I expect to hold the position to remind me of my long-term strategy.
Bias: *Disposition Effect/Selling the winners*
Description: *I feel terrible about the stocks in my account that have dropped, and I can't bring myself to sell them at a loss. I feel good about the ones that rise, so I have no problem selling those!*
Habit to adopt: *On my regular portfolio review date,* I will sell stocks that are no longer suitable or do not offer prospects of growth, regardless of their current price relative to my purchase price.
Bias:
Description:

Habit to adopt: I will

Bias:
Description:

Habit to adopt: I will

Bias:
Description:

Habit to adopt: I will

Step 7: The Key Ingredient

Think about where you are in your life and the answers you provided in the proceeding steps. The following question will help to focus your attention on how best to improve your financial situation right now. This may be a habit to integrate, a task to accomplish, or something that you wish to have, experience, or learn.

Don't compile an exhaustive list. The less complicated your answer, the more likely you'll achieve it. The point of this step is to put the most amount of effort into the single-most critical aspect of your financial affairs. If this is the only course of action you take, it will be a rewarding step.

What single accomplishment would most positively impact your financial status over the next 12 months?

Answer:

Step 8: Bringing It All Together: Your Personal Economic Values

Your particular personal economic values can be summarized by a statement you create and refer to at important inflection points throughout your life. It aligns the vision of your life's priorities with how you will execute your key goals. It is built around your strengths, and can be used to structure how you make financial decisions. It is also a reminder to focus on the key objectives that are most important to you when you're faced with unpredictable circumstances.

Your **PEV statement** will prepare you to avoid the decisions that negatively impact your financial well-being. With it, you'll be armed with the confidence that your decisions are leading you in the right direction. It should be meaningful, yet relatively brief. You can print it out on a piece of paper, frame it on your desk at home or in your office, or keep a copy where you keep important financial documents. This is a reminder of your purpose and the habits within your control to move your objectives forward.

Below are suggestions to get you started. Writing a PEV statement may seem daunting at first, but once you get started, you'll find it comes naturally. Also, remember that you can change it whenever you like, and writing an imperfect statement is better than writing nothing at all (status quo bias).

To begin, complete the following statement. Consider your list of critical values from Step 4, your risk appetite from Step 5, and your key goals from Step 2.

- *I will* __(action)__ *for* __(audience)__ *by* __(doing something)__ *to* __(achievement)__ .

You may also wish to use your own free-form statement or adapt any of these:

- *I believe that a successful life . . .*
- *To achieve my priorities, I will. . .*
- *I am confident that I . . .*
- *When financial decisions are challenging, I can consistently rely on. . .*

Chapter 5

Adopting
Unbiased Habits

The Point of Impact

The animated G.I. Joe miniseries, *A Real American Hero*, ran during the mid-1980s. The popular half-hour program follows an elite team of soldiers as they battle the evil Cobra organization in its quest for world domination. A public service announcement (PSA) notoriously ran after each episode, in which a G.I. Joe hero saves a viewer-age kid from trouble. The children found themselves caught in scenarios such as their clothing catching on fire, unthinkingly about to leave with a stranger, or lying to a friend. In each case, the G.I. Joe soldier imparts words of wisdom, telling the children what they should do to avoid these risks in the future. Invariably, the children respond, "Now we know!" And the soldier confirms that "Knowing is half the battle."

Every parent understands, however, that telling a child not to play in the street or to heed similar sound advice only goes so far. Similarly, you likely know that you should save more money each month, spend within your limits, and stay invested in the market even when it drops to disheartening lows. Yet, executing those plans when they count is difficult. You may plan to lose weight, but when you're invited out for dinner at the new French restaurant in the city, that commitment is hard to maintain.

Over the first three chapters, you learned how biased cognitive processing can lead to unintended consequences. Biases can push you to accept additional risk when you intended to limit it, induce you to stick with plans that no longer serve you, tempt you to sell your winning investments instead of holding onto them, and make other systematic errors.

Now that you are aware of how and when biases affect your choices, you may believe that you are less susceptible to these influences. Understandably, awareness of how biases impact your decisions provides a feeling of confidence that you'll make better decisions in the future. If your confidence leads you to believe that awareness is enough to prevent recurrence, however, you've fallen prey to yet another bias, aptly called the **G.I. Joe Fallacy**.

The only way to correct for these influential biases is to adopt new habits. To do that, you need to know what habits are effective and how to implement the necessary safeguards for when, inevitably, old patterns arise. The following sections outline practical habits that you can adopt for that very purpose.

The first and most critical habit is to refer to your **personal economic values (PEVs)** whenever you make important financial decisions. The second, and equally vital, is to plan when and how often to make changes to your financial strategy. Timing is everything. Plan to address your financial affairs on your timetable rather than being driven to make decisions in the midst of critical events.

Your investments and other financial affairs tend to grab your attention when there is a problem. When you need to borrow money, you've lost your job, or you've landed an unexpected windfall, your focus suddenly shifts to the crucial issue at hand.

Managing your money also becomes urgent after a dramatic spike in interest rates, an unexpected swing in the value of the currency, or when stock market volatility becomes intolerable. The worst time to make changes to your strategy is during dramatic external events. When you are under pressure or under the sway of fear or elation, the elevated stress can increase your vulnerability to the effects of biases and systematic errors in judgment.

The opposite approach – pushing off financial decisions – may also be detrimental. The often-overused excuse for delaying a financial decision is a lack of time. Yet, you can always make time for what's important. One client said that investing felt like a "false priority." He realized that it was imperative to his financial success, but he couldn't figure out where to start so he became reluctant to act. If this scenario sounds familiar, the **status quo bias** is likely to blame.

When you have too many options to consider or you are unsure of the best direction to pursue, deferral is often a more comfortable prospect. It's easier to keep doing what you're already doing, which in many cases, is to do nothing. Besides, there are always other important issues to distract you from facing the ones that are complicated or time-consuming.

Setting a schedule to address financial choices is a savvy approach to effectively manage your financial affairs. Scheduling specific times to manage critical decisions will increase your commitment to address important matters, especially if you arrange these meetings with a professional advisor. You will not only increase the likelihood of getting the job done, but also avoid in-the-moment decision errors induced by trying to form choices during hectic experiences.

Establish your financial decision-dates on a schedule that is recurring, but infrequent enough that you do not feel overwhelmed, and you aren't tempted to alter your course too often. If you know that your decision-date is coming up, it relieves pressure to address any important issue that may feel prodigious at the time that it arises. By scheduling a predictable date to address your finances, you can often defer otherwise transactional decisions to a time that is less volatile. Also, financial choices are less likely to languish unattended when specific times are dedicated to the cause.

Consider setting a date to review your investments annually. Instead of making rash changes to your investment strategy when you hear about a drop in the stock market on the morning news, you'll be able to calmly review your objectives when emotion is less likely to influence your decisions. Bring your written PEVs to the meeting, or review them before making any changes to your plans. This will remind you of your future goals prior to making changes and ensure that any alterations are in line with your objectives.

Limit the number of decisions you make over your lifetime by aligning your choices with your values and goals. It should be obvious that the fewer choices that you need to make, the less chance you'll have of making a judgment error. If you have five choices to make, the greatest number of wrong ones is five.

The more effective your choices are, the less often you'll need to change them. You can't wander too far off course if you consistently apply your values and critical long-term goals. Visualizing your endgame and keeping your eye on your personal economic values will inevitably limit the number of twists and turns along the way, and ultimately reduce the number of decisions you'll face. That doesn't mean that you can't have short-term plans. It means that decisions associated with your overarching objectives will persistently lead you toward your goals.

For example, imagine that your dream is to save $75,000 for a family vacation property over seven years. You map out the plan to deposit $600 per month, which means that you'll need roughly 8% return to get there. There is only one asset class to do that kind of heavy lifting. However, equities come with more volatility than other assets, which can lead to **loss aversion**. Reactions to loss aversion can induce you to consider selling your stake or discontinue your contributions when investment markets become volatile, derailing your seven-year goal. If you set this plan in place during your scheduled decision time, and commit to leaving it unaltered until your next decision date, you'll be better equipped to avoid biased decisions during a crisis.

The more consistent you can be to this process, the less often your choices will lead to regrettable outcomes. Make decisions when you are calm and focused, rather than in the throes of emotion. This will lessen the influences of bias, external factors, and uncontrollable events. Scheduling them will hold you to a set timing rather than the whims of market fluctuations, and ensure that important tasks are addressed. You'll benefit most when you're in control of this process.

External events can influence you to behave in ways that are counterproductive or prevent you from achieving what you really want. If a regular payment into a managed, diversified equity portfolio is your plan, keep up your contributions regardless of market conditions. Sticking to your key objectives isn't always easy when short-run situations are unnerving. Regardless of the current economy, you purchase more shares with each dollar that you contribute when prices are low. The more shares you have, the more your wealth increases as the share prices rise.

You spent a meaningful amount of time and effort in the last chapter to discover your underlying beliefs and dreams about the future. You wrote down the skills you're comfortable with and listed the types of expertise you want to outsource. You considered the critical question of what is holding you back from making important monetary decisions. Also, you determined how you feel about risk, which is a vital tool that you can use to describe your tolerance for volatility to financial professionals that you work with.

You've uncovered your underlying belief systems about wealth and stated the key elements you need to move forward. Now you're ready to act, with the benefit of having developed your PEVs.

If you've ever chosen not to keep chocolate in your pantry to tempt you, you've managed the impact of your natural biases. The first bias you learned to avoid is the G.I. Joe Fallacy. Knowing is not enough to create meaningful change. The second is how and when to best address your financial affairs, with scheduled decision dates to implement and maintain your PEVs and critical goals. You can now reach your financial objectives with fewer judgment errors by scheduling financial reviews and applying your PEVs.

Don't Take It Personally

"Whatever you do, don't follow my advice. Whenever I buy a stock, the price drops."

A Schoolteacher

We often take random or unforeseen events to heart. It's also comforting to defend past unsuccessful decisions to sooth the emotional discomfort they evoke. **Hindsight bias** propagates feeling of regret and leads you to think that if you could have foreseen unpredictable events, you could have acted differently. Too often, you'll feel angst when you're compelled to stick to plans to which you've committed time or money (**sunk-cost bias**), despite those plans no longer serving your needs or desires. Comparably, investment losses can cause anguish, and lead you to seek higher risks in the hopes of making back the difference (loss aversion and **break-even effect**).

External forces will influence how you feel, even though they are random or unpreventable. You will be inclined to see patterns when there aren't any, as discussed in the section about the **gambler's fallacy**. Unpredictable events are called unpredictable for a reason. Yet, you'll be inclined to find justification and draw conclusions about the risks you've taken and choices you've made that were later impacted by unknowable external events.

When a company announces a surprise merger, you may feel very happy even though you had nothing to do with the announcement or the resulting price appreciation. Nor should the increased value validate your investment decision since the information was unknown. You couldn't have based your decision on it, yet, its common to hold onto that sensation.

Even though you aren't responsible for unknowable information, unexpected events still cause feelings of euphoria or regret. To deal with pleasant feelings, it's natural to be quick to take responsibility for successful decision. When your investment rises, it's easy to believe that you had a hand in it, at least in part. For negative events, it's more palatable to pawn off poor outcomes on other factors. When an investment value drops, it's easy to disavow your decision to invest, and blame something or someone else for why you held it.

Good decisions – rooted in analysis and research – as well as poorly formed choices can both result in profits or losses. However, the sooner you realize that you cannot control random events, the more easily you'll be able to disregard the price gyrations of your investment portfolio. The sooner you accept that market fluctuations and price changes aren't about you, the happier you'll be.

It is important to recognize that you naturally identify patterns that make events feel predictable, even when those relationships don't exist. As the number of variables increases, the predictability of future outcomes decreases. Forecasts about the stock market, foreign currency exchange rates, commodity prices, or the economy are substantially unreliable. Long-term economic trends tend to be more consistent than short-term trends because of the general nature of economic growth; however, the infinite number of possibilities make the future largely unknowable.

It is this unknowability that you want to control, yet cannot. Don't take random events and outcomes personally. They don't have anything to do with you. You are only responsible for forming well-thought-out decisions and limiting errors in judgment. The best option is to set out a path aligned with your PEVs that leads to the future you desire, and steadfastly stick to your plan.

Quantify Your Returns

"I haven't made any gains in my RRSP except for the money that I've contributed myself!"

Overheard at lunch

Both recent and emotional events are indelibly etched in your memory-bank. When you rely on your recollection, your decisions will be overly influenced by these ready details due to both the **recency effect** and **availability bias,** discussed in Chapter 2.

Your memory of dramas such as the Great Depression, World War II, the 1999 technology bubble, the 2008 financial crisis, or the 2020 pandemic undoubtedly influence your future investment outlook. If you participated in the economy or investment markets during any of these volatile episodes, you will likely have imagined what you'd do if you could have avoided it, and you will establish mental notes of what to avoid in the future based on these events.

The recency effect and availability bias make it easy to neglect long-term investment return data and focus on recent trends instead. You likely can't recall what it feels like to be a child waking up from a nap, but you know how it felt when you woke up this morning. We are psychologically built to rely on examples that are easy to recall, thinking that they are more relevant. When markets drop like your stomach at the crest of a roller-coaster, a history of long-term steady performance can be drowned out by the momentary volatility.

Rather than rely on a memory – which is partial to recent or dramatic information – it's more reliable to keep a ledger and a calculator handy to track your investment returns. A simple numeric tally can recalibrate your viewpoint and ensure that you have a clear picture rooted in fact. If you thought that your current investment strategy isn't delivering on your objectives because volatility has distorted your recollection of the long-run investment returns, dust off your calculator or your Excel spreadsheet and write down the numbers. Your investment provider will also be able to provide a history of your contributions, withdrawals, and numeric performance.

A simple approach is to keep a spreadsheet. Label the top of each column with the calendar year, beginning value, contributions and withdrawals, the ending value, and your percentage return, as in the example below.

Year	Beginning Value	Contributions/ Withdrawals	Ending Value	% Gain/Loss

Use a relative performance number – a percentage return – rather than relying on the absolute increase in dollars to reduce distortions of your perception. If you believe that you've always made the best returns on real estate rather than your RRSP or 401(k), consider the fact that the bigger the quantity of your investment, the higher the dollar value increases. Although an increase of $50,000 seems like a good return, if your initial investment is $850,000, then a $50,000 gain is only 5.88%. The relative increase of 9% in your savings may be substantially more even if the dollars invested are much less.

Also, if you borrow money for part of your purchase, the leverage enhances the growth. Borrowing to invest in your investment portfolio will produce the same effect as borrowing to buy a home. Both the size of the investment and the leverage typical of real estate increase the perception that you're earning a greater return.

Take care to avoid anchoring by resisting temptation to track your portfolio peaks. Climax values are almost impossible to forget. Setting a high-water mark can cause an unnecessary visceral disappointment despite earning good overall returns.

Other than for calculating taxes, past prices are irrelevant and your future investment opportunities have nothing to do with your initial investment cost. As tempting as it is to fix a dollar value as the next goalpost, you'll be happier to know that you achieved a fair return. Instead of relying on a fallacious guess of your performance, keep track and calculate your returns to ensure that you're on the right track.

Keep a Journal of Investment Decisions

"I've seen this before. A decline in oil prices will result in a depreciation of the Canadian dollar."

Anonymous Analyst

Everyone has a natural tendency to want to be right. You may even subconsciously select information and search for details that align with your outlook. Your bias is to prefer supportive details and disregard conflicting data. It should be obvious that placing a heavy reliance on only certain aspects of a story will result in a skewed viewpoint, despite your best intentions.

Imagine that your investment advisor recommends selling shares of a company that you've held for a long time; one that you're fond of. Upon reading the research report that is the basis for her recommendation, you note that the situation may not be as dire as she predicts. You come to the company's defense and cite several positive comments in the report that you've fished out. However, relying on selective information that confirms what we want to believe – **confirmation bias** – can lead to unprofitable decisions or can put you in the way of unnecessary risk.

It isn't easy to remain open-minded. If you identify with the confirmation bias, you're in good company. The best way to avoid these tendencies is to maintain a diary of facts about your investment decisions. Prior to making an investment, list both the reasons in favor of investing and reasons not to invest. This will help you to achieve a more sober view about the opportunity. If you proceed, make notes about how the investment meets your objectives so that you can reflect on the decision if economic conditions change. If the share price drops soon after your initial investment, you can avoid the distress of hindsight bias by recalling the compelling reasons you had to initiate the investment in the first place.

> *"The oil stock I bought last summer kept dropping. Why did I buy it when I knew that the world is moving to renewable resources!"*
>
> Anonymous Investor

If an asset is no longer suitable, you should sell it, regardless of how long you've held it or what you paid for it. That may be easier said than done, but keeping a journal will help you maintain objectivity. You'll be better equipped to see when your reasons to investment deteriorate, rather than choosing an exit strategy based on price changes or perceived patterns induced by the gambler's fallacy, loss aversion, or anchoring.

This process is as simple as keeping a notebook; however, there are several electronic diary options that make sorting and retrieving data more efficient. Date each entry for reference. Limit your entries to critical factors so that the task isn't so onerous that it prevents you from keeping your notes. Also, list both the good and bad developments that will prompt you to dispose of an investment. With those three pieces of information, your decisions will be increasingly impartial. This will help lessen the number of biased or unnecessary transactions that you make.

The Power of SMT

In 1998, at a medium-sized manufacturing company, employees were invited to meet with a financial planner. Each employee was told that they were under-saving by a wide margin and the planner suggested that they should be saving at least 15% of their salary. Most of the employees were shocked and responded that such a high savings rate was impossible. Reducing their paycheck would mean that they couldn't meet their current expenses. The advisor then suggested that the employee increase their savings rate by 5%. And, a quarter of the employees agreed to this strategy. Of those who were still unable to commit, the advisor offered a save-more-tomorrow (SMT) option. When their salary increased, so would their savings rate. An overwhelming majority of employees agreed to adopt the SMT plan.

During the study, employees who didn't meet with the financial specialist didn't change their savings rates. The group that initially increased their savings by 5% typically didn't add any more thereafter. In comparison, individuals who agreed to increase their contributions in lockstep with their salary had a savings rate almost 4% higher than those who started saving right away.[1]

Savings plans often invoke a biased resistance. While you realize that saving protects your future, you still suffer a sense of loss when it cuts into what you can spend today. The SMT reduces the psychological resistance to saving by deferring it to a future date – which is far more agreeable – while maintaining a commitment. It also doesn't erode your current purchasing power because you haven't enjoyed spending the increase in salary yet.

Another way to apply the SMT is by increasing your mortgage payment each time you earn a raise. Even if the increased payment amount is nominal, every additional penny is applied to the outstanding principal. The less principle you owe, the lower your interest costs, and the larger portion of each future payment further reduces what you owe.

For young people, the first few years of financial independence are the most financially difficult. Saving at this early stage, however, has the most significant impact on the overall amount you'll need to save from your earnings. The sooner you start, the less you will need to contribute to your *future-you* by a stunningly wide margin. Starting at age 20, saving $100 per month at 6% return will amass to $275,599 once you're 65. If you postpone saving until you're 30, you will only accumulate $142,471. That missed decade of contributing $100 per month amounts to a mere $12,000. A small price to pay for an extra $133,128!

Ad hoc savings plans – as opposed to those that automatically generate each month – are the most difficult to execute successfully. Not only does loss aversion reduce your willingness to manually deduct funds from your bank account, **overconfidence** and the gambler's fallacy can also thwart your strategy if you begin to believe that you can time the market. Moreover, emotions make it difficult to invest in a plan when investment prices are volatile.

Automated savings plans are significantly better than improvised investing. Scheduled contributions to an investment with variable market prices work to reduce your adjusted cost base by buying securities at various prices over time. Also, routine contributions reduce your biased interference in the plan. First, establish your savings to align with your key objectives and your personal economic values. Then leave those well-constructed plans to play out. The less you are involved in daily financial decisions thereafter, the less likely it is that you'll make an error in judgment, and the less stress you'll feel overall. Set it and forget it.

The only improvement on an automated savings plan from your bank account is one funded directly from your employer. You may feel reluctant to give up any of your current spending power once it's in your bank account. But, you can reduce the impact of this sense of loss aversion by contributing before your payroll is in your hands. Many employees report that over time, they don't even notice that it's missing. Also, direct savings plans can help to defer income taxes. Contributions by your employer directly to a registered retirement savings account may also reduce the amount of taxes withheld by your employer. That keeps more money available for you to invest.

Once you have a savings plan that hits critical mass, where it noticeably grows from both your contributions and from investment returns, feelings generated by loss aversion subside because of the mounting pot of savings. Over the last several decades, I've seen clients turn from reluctant savers into enthusiastic ones once the threshold of their investment pool is substantial enough to grow at a noticeable pace. As the absolute amount that your portfolio has grown becomes obvious, the feelings of loss seem to reverse.

When Nobel Laureate Richard Thaler and his colleague, Shlomo Benartzi, created the save-more-tomorrow plan, they were onto something important. The plan considers critical aspects of our natural biases. It is easier to commit to self-control restrictions that will happen in the future. Not only is it easier to start your diet tomorrow, but they found that people are more inclined to pledge to save in the future, too. It is more comfortable to commit to a savings plan that begins *soon* rather than one that starts right now.[2]

Negotiations

"I can't believe that they made such a low-ball offer to buy our home! Who do they think they are?"

A Toronto Homeowner

We value our stuff more highly than the amount we'd be willing to pay to attain it. As described in Chapter 1, people are more likely to keep something than to buy it if they don't own it already.

Stocks that trade minute to minute on an exchange have a valuation that is easy to see. When it comes to illiquid assets, however, determining a fair price is more difficult due to this **endowment effect**. Obtaining a third-party evaluation is one way to reduce this discrepancy. In fact, with investments such as real estate, it is worth obtaining more than one arm's-length estimate to determine the value of a property.

During negotiations to trade assets, both the buyer and seller are affected by anchoring to the list price as well as the first bid. Anchoring sets the stage for the final price in all negotiations. If the list price or offer is too high or the initial bid is too low, you're better to walk away than to try to adjust the negotiations by countering with an outrageous response in the opposite direction. The further apart the buyer and seller are, the less likely an agreement will be reached.

When you engage in a negotiation to buy something, consider that your first bid is aimed to achieve two things: anchor your opponent to a low figure, and discover how much they're willing to move from their listed price. Your initial bid must be reasonable enough to be taken seriously, but low enough to achieve your objectives. Once you have their counteroffer, you can better judge whether you can reach an agreement on price. Then, you can make your last-and-best offer. The more haggling, however, the greater likelihood that one of you will be influenced by the process and will talk yourself into amending your decided final price. The **proportional money effect** can make bargaining in small amounts lead to larger losses than you'd otherwise be willing to accept.

Just Pick One

An egregious number of new employees neglect to sign up for employer-sponsored benefits. The reasons for this range from being too busy with the new job to complete the paperwork, to a lack of understanding the options offered.

When you don't know how much to commit to an employment savings plan, choosing an option with a dart board is better than stammering until you've decided nothing. If you don't like your decision, at least your contributions have begun, and you can always make a new choice later, once you better understand the choices. There is no pressure to make a perfect selection or to maximize an idealized benefit, especially when it stalls you from setting up the plan altogether. It is critical to begin a savings plan as soon as possible, since the amount of time that you invest is as important as how much you contribute, especially when the employer matches your contributions or contributes on your behalf.

When your company offers to match your investment, there is usually a limit on how much you can contribute. In the absence of compelling reasons to select any other amount, choose the amount that maximizes the company's subsidy. The more money that comes effortlessly, the better. Collect as much effortless money as you can, as soon as you can.

Selecting a suitable strategy is another stumbling block that can delay or prevent investing. If the bevy of options makes your eyes glaze over, remember that making a decision that isn't quite right is better than not deciding anything at all. It would be unusual for a pension plan or employer-sponsored plan to provide particularly risky options. However, if your company offers the opportunity to invest in the shares of the company you work for, recall that **familiarity bias** may influence you to choose that option. Consider, instead, how your current income is already exposed to economic changes that affect the company you work for. If you invest your savings in the same company from which you get paid, you're concentrating your risk. When General Motors Company, Enron Corporation, and Sears, Roebuck and Co. each declared bankruptcy, the employees who had all of their savings in their pension plan didn't only lose future wages. They also lost the pension benefits and deferred profit-sharing plans built over many years. If the only option is to buy the shares of the company you work for, consider moving your savings into a diversified portfolio after the vesting period, as long as you are not subject to realizing significant taxes when making the switch.

Company-sponsored investment plans often provide a variety of investment selections such as equity, bond and balanced funds. You may be better off to select one fund instead of combining them. Allocating 50% of your investment into an equity fund and 50% into a balanced fund means that you have 75% in stocks and 25% in bonds. Each of these funds is already diversified and investing all your funds into one of these mandates will not result in a drastic error. If you're not sure which one to choose, selecting a balanced fund is a moderate approach, and relatively suitable for most people.

When you have a long investment time horizon, and you can be patient through the ups and downs of a full economic cycle, investing in a managed, diversified equity or stock portfolio may be suitable. If you need to access your money soon, however, it is often smart to be more conservative.

Commencing the savings plan is more critical than the investment choice that you select. When the prospects of a financial decision are daunting, find a professional that you trust to help you decide. Regardless, participating in any fund in any quantity is better than not choosing anything at all. Henry Ford wasn't talking about signing up for a pension plan with a new employer when he said, "Indecision is often worse than the wrong action." Nevertheless, he is spot-on.

Automate, Outsource, and Schedule

"Boy, that new cell phone service is much cheaper, but they probably don't have adequate coverage."

Overheard

Take a few minutes to review Chapter 4, Step 6: *What is holding you back?* and Step 3: *What are your financial skills?* Highlight the items you can automate, outsource, or schedule reminders to complete.

The adage, "the devil you know is better than the one you don't," expresses why people prefer to keep with the status quo. The hassle of making changes, the effort of investigating new options, and the confusion of alternatives can stall you from making necessary changes to make improvements. Cellular phone providers regularly adjust the plans that they offer to align with changing bandwidth demands and capacity to remain competitive in the marketplace. Often, new plans are more affordable, offer better services, or both. When was the last time you reviewed your phone plan or investigated other carriers? For many people, it was several years ago because it is much easier to stay with the arrangement that you already have.

The plague of inertia is hardwired in all of us, even the most motivated. Whether you lack gumption, interest, or you fear taking the wrong action, status quo bias is at work. Commonly used scapegoats carry powerful lures that impede you from achieving the success you desire. How many times have you kicked yourself for not getting around to doing something that would have paid off handsomely, and left you with feelings of regret generated from hindsight bias?

One of the best ways to manage motivation is not to rely on yourself at all. In the digital age, you can automate many regular financial decisions. The more often you must intervene and manage financial choices, the more often you are at risk of bias decisions and judgment error.

Use technology for each possible instance. Automation is one of the most straightforward functions you can use to your advantage. New processes are devised regularly and made available before you're even aware that they exist.

By building mechanical structures in your life, you can simplify many responsibilities. It also reduces ongoing tedious maintenance, limits your chores, and liberates your mind from unnecessary transactions. You'll have more time, less stress, and better financial results by automating a number of investment decisions. Consider setting up schedules to rebalance your portfolio, make investment contributions, transfer regular payments, and manage contract renewals with a diary notation or with an outside service provider who will execute your transaction. For example, when your car insurance is set to expire, either put a note in your calendar or have your insurance provider set up a system to call or email you with the options for your renewal, the week prior to the expiry date of last year's coverage.

Contributions to an investment plan are always best when set at regular intervals, directly from your company's payroll or through a recurring electronic contribution. Remove the risk of bias on your investment contributions by setting them up to generate electronically, without you having to intervene. Like taking cough syrup, if you think about how bad it tastes, you may resist despite the benefits.

Automate the process of resetting the amount you hold in each type of investment, or at least schedule a reminder to rebalance your portfolio periodically. This strategy is called tactical asset allocation. Pick a frequency that makes sense for the volatility of your portfolio. For a very volatile portfolio, rebalancing each quarter is not uncommon. For low-volatility investments, you may only want to rebalance your portfolio annually or semiannually. Your diary must include the amount you'll allocate to each asset, the steps to process any changes, how to implement the change, and the contact information for the people who need to make changes. Or, ensure that your investment professional has an automated process in place.

Automate fixed costs. Most banks offer scheduled payments and automatic money transfers. Establish an account for fixed costs and move those funds into that account each payday. Then, have all of your fixed expenses automatically deducted from that account. You'll find that this will fit into your natural inclination for **mental accounting**, to segregate your money.

For processes that can't be completely automated, use an electronic diary to remind you of all the steps to execute what is needed to complete the task. Stick to one electronic system and be selective – only set up recurring events and essential tasks.

Don't fall into the trap of setting up future reminders for tasks that you don't want to do today. If you don't want to do them now, you likely won't want to do them in the future either, and they will bog down your process.

Include all the steps, resources, and helpful information needed to execute the entire job so that you aren't stalled by looking for other details. For example, if you have a reminder to meet with your financial advisor for your annual investment review, include their contact information, where to park, what to bring to the meeting, and critical questions to ask – and of course, bring a copy of your PEVs and your **investment policy statement (IPS)**, which we will develop in the sections ahead. By including these details, you will have fewer stumbling blocks that will interfere with following through with the task.

Outsourcing is another option. Some tasks require advanced processes or expertise. In this case, it's worth considering hiring a professional to manage them for you. Set tasks in motion that others can do more efficiently; they will also be affected less by bias. Financial processes can be executed sooner, more easily, and less affected by bias. You'll be able to devote your extra time to more complex issues or enjoyable pastimes.

Stop Checking Your Investments

People are generally risk-averse. We are about twice as sensitive to losses as gains of the same nominal amount. Unfortunately, that also means that it hurts almost twice as much to lose one dollar compared to the joy of gaining one. So, when there are as many days that stock prices rise as days that they fall, and the pain of loss outweighs our enjoyment of gains, it's easy to see why so many investors avoid stocks despite higher long-term returns.

Since 1900, stocks have added an average 4.2% per year more than Treasury bills to investment performance, and 3.2% more than a market-weighted bond portfolio, across 21 countries worldwide.[3] Nevertheless, owning shares is a sickening prospect for some investors because the ups and downs instill fear and feelings of discontent. It's a natural predisposition to believe that you are losing ground the more often you look at your investments.

There are two conventional methods to manage the emotional distress of loss aversion generated by stock market volatility. One is to diversify part of your portfolio into securities with an opposite (uncorrelated) price movement. When one investment class moves up and the other moves down, they generally balance each other. This diversification effectively smooths out the overall impact of price changes on your portfolio to reduce the swings you experience. This strategy provides an added opportunity to buy asset classes that have dropped with ones that have risen, assuming that you have the stomach to execute such a trade.

The other approach is to stop checking your investments.

The frequency of checking your investments increases the opportunity to worry about changes in prices and other micro-events in the economic or political landscape. When your investments are up, you feel a little lighthearted. When they are down, you console yourselves with *reasons,* and coach yourselves not to worry. The more significant the loss, the more emotional the response.

More importantly, worry causes distress and can induce investors to make unnecessary transactions. The more often you transact, the more you lose on transaction fees and the spreads between the bid and ask prices. Also, each time you trade, you increase the number of occasions to make trading slip-ups that result in further erosion. Most importantly, however, the risk of judgment errors are higher for no other reason than the increased frequency of trading.

Recall that the **disposition effect** is the inclination to sell your winning stocks prematurely and hold onto the losers in the hope that they will return to earlier values. For tax reasons and profitability, you can benefit measurably by guarding against this predisposition.

Emotional responses to loss aversion, overconfidence, disposition effect, and other behavioral biases lead to increased trading. Checking your investments frequently:

• leads to panic, which leads to selling.
• leads to doubt, which leads to buying and selling.
• leads to dread, which leads to canceling contributions.
• leads to anxiety, which leads to unnecessary transactions.
• leads to transactions, which increase the possibility of making an error.

In each decade since 1930, missing the best 10 days in the market would have reduced your total profit to a paltry 91%. Comparatively, leaving your investment untouched for the entire period would have produced 14,962%.[4]

It may sound counterintuitive to stop checking your investments. This strategy doesn't mean letting your assets languish like an old forgotten castle with the sofas covered in dusty cotton covers and chandeliers draped in cobwebs. With a professionally managed investment solution, reviewing your investments once a year is likely ample.

Many government officials and other influential people must place their investments into a blind trust to avoid conflicts of interest and insider trading. In the process, government officials avoid biases in the policies that they pursue in public office. The officers select a professional or team of professionals to manage their affairs while they are not privy to what they own. Why couldn't you take the same approach if it alleviates the discomforts of emotional investment-fatigue?

Mathematically, the longer the periods between investment reports, the smoother the reported returns are. If you paid attention to the broad stock market index once every 10 years, you might calmly note that it has appreciated every time you review it by a comfortable amount. If, over the same period, you avoid the daily market news, you may not sense any cause for concern at all. In retrospect, even the financial crisis of 2008 is a small blip in the upward march of the stock market, despite being a reported catastrophe at the time.

People who decide how much to allocate to stocks versus bonds in their pension fund tend to choose a higher allocation to stocks when shown one- and five-year returns than those who are shown monthly returns.[5] Investors monitoring their reports monthly, naturally observe frequent periods of losses since that is the nature of these investments. Increased volatility deters people from investing in stocks.

By measuring loss aversion against stock market volatility, Benartzi and Thaler suggest that investors should not review their stock portfolios any more than once a year. They found that even long-term investors review their portfolios frequently, to their detriment. They argue that yearly is a natural period to report investment returns. After all, we are already acclimated to attend to our tax filing once a year, so perhaps this is the time to review your investment performance too.[6]

Suppose that you are risk averse. Checking your portfolio less frequently can allow you to invest in higher volatility investments with better returns because the volatility isn't as alarming. Even risk-averse investors are more willing to invest a higher proportion of their investment portfolio to equities if they look at their investments less often. In that case, checking your portfolio less often may produce better performance with less grief and lower stress.

Moreover, you can avoid the tax complications and counterintuitive losses associated with the disposition effect. Deferring capital gains taxes keeps more money in your hands, and as we pointed out in Chapter 2, profitable stocks tend to continue to outperform.

Establish Investment Constraints

Hi Coreen,

It's RRSP time again. My accountant recommends that I top up my contributions, but last year, the stocks in my RRSP didn't do very well. In comparison, my rental properties keep rising. I wanted to know what you think the next year will bring and whether it would make more sense to pay down the mortgage on my rental properties or buy the RRSP.

Thanks, John.

***

Hello John,

That's an excellent question. Given your high-income level as a real estate agent, you pay taxes at the top marginal tax rate. At this tax rate, about half of the money you contribute to your RRSP* is money that you'd otherwise pay to the Canada Revenue Agency (CRA). For every dollar you invest, only 50 cents of it is yours, and the other 50 cents is the taxes you would otherwise owe to CRA. You get to choose whether you give it to them now or invest it for a while and give it to them later. Think of your RRSP contribution partly as an interest-free loan from the Canadian Government to earn additional investment income before retirement.

Also, remember that the value of a dollar diminishes each year because the cost of living increases every year, devaluing purchasing power over time. Therefore, a dollar you pay in taxes today is costlier than if you pay it in the future. Moreover, you will have stopped earning employment income when you retire, so your tax bracket will likely be lower.

You will be reducing your mortgage with after-tax dollars, meaning that you'll only have roughly half of what you will contribute to your RRSP. Also, the advantage of reducing your mortgage is limited to the interest rate that you're paying, which is low.

Both capital markets and real estate markets oscillate at different times. One is driven by business growth, and the second is primarily affected by interest rates. Historically, however, equities outperform real estate over long periods, including the most recent real estate boom.

All to say, I side with your accountant.

Sincerely, Coreen

★★★

*For American readers, an RRSP is comparable to a 401(k) as a tax deferral for retirement savings. Although the rates are different, the same principles apply as in the example above.

It stands to reason that investors tend to overweight investments they know well, sometimes for no other reason than their personal experience and comfort level. Buying shares of a company solely because you use their products is more common that you may think. For example, the predisposition to overweight your portfolio in bank stocks because you worked in finance for most of your life is because you've fallen under the spell of the familiarity bias. Similarly, the home bias compels you to gravitate toward investments in your region or country.

John, the real estate agent, who penned the email above, would benefit from enforcing guidelines for diversification in his *investment policy statement* (which we will construct together in a following section). This step will help to avoid familiarity bias.

Stick to Your Plan

"Everyone is buying gold stocks. There must be a good reason."

Biased Investor

Investors sometimes defer to mimicking another investors' behavior and fall into herd mentality. It isn't a new phenomenon to take the word of a business news anchor, internet influencer, or even your seemingly knowledgeable Uber driver from the airport. You may find yourself considering the prospects of the opportunity they brought to your attention – availability bias at work. However, once you believe it is a decent idea, you will also be influenced by confirmation bias to seek corroborating evidence. We have a natural tendency to find research to support an investment idea rather than discredit it.

Have you ever thought that if an investment was good enough for a famously successful investor, like Warren Buffett, that it's good enough for you? Or, were you inspired to start adding oil stocks to your portfolio based on a conversation you had with someone that sounded intelligent about the subject? These are common biases that can lead you off-track. Even a good investment idea can change course. Mr. Buffett isn't planning to call you before he sells the security he was discussing on the interview you watched.

Determine the quality of investments you're prepared to invest in and the criteria those investments possess. Adding constraints to your investment strategy will limit exposure to unsuitable options that don't align with your personal economic values.

Reframing Decisions

"ABC reported earnings per share of $1.18 versus the expected earnings of only $1.03. An eighteen percent earnings beat is fantastic!"

Newscaster

The delivery of information influences our perception and, ultimately, how we act on it. If a company announces surprise upside earnings of $3.87 cents per share, it is undoubtedly positive news. But how would the sentiment change if the company earned $4.85 per share last year?

When is a win a win?

When it isn't already expected by market participants and priced in to the security's trading price.

Of course, a sales pitch never acknowledges the negatives of a product. You would never learn that the dishwasher detergent doesn't work very well in certain types of dishwashing machines. A sales strategy is meant to overwhelm the audience with positive aspects. We, as consumers, have come to expect it. Nevertheless, those of us suffering from **confirmation bias** are only too happy to let the good news flood over us and guide us to the supermarket to pick up a package.

When reviewing investment options, *framing* influences the way you tend to view options. A sales pitch can pander to your desires and omit shortcomings with the stroke of a pen. A 20% opportunity to profit sounds a lot better than an 80% chance of failure. To compound the issue, research found that older adults may be more susceptible to **framing effects** due to well-developed emotional frames and immediate reactions to financial gains and losses.[7]

Taking matters into your own hands is a valuable process. For weighty decisions that sound like a good solution, consider writing a pros and cons lists of equal length to help calibrate your viewpoint. Another approach is to write an anti-sales pitch to highlight the counterpoints before you commit to it. For example, take the statement that the portfolio has a 40% expectation that it may grow by 12%. You could also point out that the portfolio has a 60% chance to return less than 12%, and that it also may decline in value. Whenever you find your spirits excessively heightened, douse the flames of excitement prior to making the investment.

The option to invest may be bona fide. The best way to avoid regret is to make your choice with your eyes wide open by seeing the ugly underside of the investment's belly.

No Safety in Numbers

"Paid off mom's house with #GameStop #profits"

Random Tweet

Safety in numbers is the general principle that if others are doing it, you're probably on the right track. A gazelle's survival as it crosses the plains shrouded by the herd literally depends on it. Following the group may feel like a good way to avoid blunders with investment decisions, too. After all, if everyone else is doing it that way, it must be right. With investing, however, this conventional wisdom often comes at a cost.

Ironically, as an investment gains appeal, prices rise and potential profits decrease. Despite this truth, investors are compelled to join a throng of others in their successes. The bigger the profits already won by other investors, the more enticing the idea becomes, and the less profitable and higher risk it becomes for you.

The social appeal of participation in the crowd comes at a financial cost if you don't get in early enough. Your timing is critical, and you will often be too late if it's popular. For example, when a popular blog or newsletter recommends a particular stock, they typically don't recommend buying at a specific price. They just recommend it. However, it's obvious that buying a good company at a reasonable price is a better investment than buying the same shares at a much higher price. The price that you pay is critical to whether the trade is profitable or not.

Maintaining rigorous independence is not as difficult or time consuming as it may sound. When buying any asset class with variable prices, it's critical to know what relative value you'll accept and when the price no longer makes sense. Stress induced by the ever-changing outlook of mob-mentality, however, can be eradicated when your underlying beliefs anchor your investment decisions.

Money Doesn't Care Where It Came From

"I'd rather get a tax refund every year rather than owe CRA!"

A Baby Boomer

Mental accounting is the process of segregating money into categories. We do this naturally, generally assigning funds based on how we acquired it or how we plan to spend it. If you have set up bank accounts, envelopes, or mason jars to allocate how much to set aside for your housing costs, for example, you've used this natural tendency to your advantage. In fact, it is an effective budgeting strategy. You can more easily track what's left over for discretionary spending by setting aside the amount you need to meet your essential fixed expenses first.

While you're at it, set up accounts and automatic savings for the important goals you set out in your PEVs. If you fund these plans regularly, it's more likely that they will happen.

Since your mental accounts are sticky, take care to limit the use of them, and the amount of money that you assign to each category. Once you designate funds to a particular purpose, reallocating it isn't as simple as you'd imagine. Your natural tendency is to dogmatically bind cash to the plans you set out when it could be better directed to more valuable goals that arise. Sure, the vacation is an important goal, but applying your money toward an unexpected credit card debt instead of leaving it in the bank account or envelope with *vacation* written across the front could save you a meaningful amount of interest costs. Paying for expenses that you've already consumed, however, doesn't feel very rewarding – certainly not as rewarding as setting aside funds for something that you'll be able to enjoy in the near future. Also, you may harbor the feeling that once the payment to earlier debt is paid, the money is gone, and then think that the trip is in jeopardy. However, whether you pay off the debt or hoard the funds in the separate account, you still have the same amount of money available to you at the end of the day.

Unexpected money is often allocated to discretionary spending, leaving employment income to do the heavy lifting of regular expenses. We tend to feel different about dollars earned at work than we do about a windfall, such as cash in a birthday card. We aren't acclimated to thinking about money that you receive from different sources as equal, but it is. It is ironically unnatural to apply your money evenly. The logic of spending employment income on regular expenses and windfalls to *extras* is unfounded since money can potentially be applied wherever it's needed. Money is fungible. It doesn't care where it came from or what it is being spent on. Neither should you.

Instead of spending windfalls on discretionary wants and allocating employment income to the necessary expenses, consider putting money where it provides you the best advantage. Helping you to meet your necessary costs more easily can feel surprisingly rewarding, reducing interest costs and stress. The less money you owe, the less interest you pay, and the more money you can keep for yourself from your payroll or any windfalls.

Consider setting aside the money you need to meet your fixed costs and critical goals set out in Chapter 4, each month, by first determining those quantities. Assign any money you receive (windfall or employment) to meet these obligations first. Then, when you receive other money, regardless of the source, spend or save at liberty.

Craft Your Personal Investment Policy Statement (IPS)

Virginia Apgar graduated from the Columbia University College of Physicians and Surgeons in 1933. After acquiring a laundry-list of accreditations, she became the first anesthesiology professor at the college and ultimately directed the department of anesthesiology at Columbia-Presbyterian Medical Center. Her interest in treating newborns led to the development of a standardized process to determine whether additional medical care is required after birth. Her checklist assesses heart rate, muscle tone, and other simple yet vital indicators of the newborn child. Today the Apgar test is used across many developed nations. It has become an essential tool for evaluating the viability of babies shortly after delivery.[8]

Atul Gawande is a surgeon in New York and a Harvard Medical School professor, among other accolades. His book, *The Checklist Manifesto, How to Get Things Right* (2009), discusses the benefits of adopting standardization – such as a checklist – to reduce human error when executing critical or complicated processes. The book became a *New York Times* hardcover nonfiction bestseller.

The success of the Apgar Score and the famous *Checklist Manifesto* are testaments to how well checklists work to increase consistent desired outcomes.

An investment policy statement (IPS) is the most important checklist for your financial health. It's a written set of guidelines for your investment decisions. It provides a consistent approach to your investment decisions that aligns with your PEVs. It is also an effective tool to communicate your preferences with investment and other financial professionals. Establishing an IPS is critical to ensure that your message is clear and that your decisions remains consistent. When market conditions and other influences stimulate biased or emotional decision-making, a written document can counteract impressions of random events and direct you through variable forces. It can also be a yardstick to monitor and evaluate your progress toward your financial objectives.

Think of an IPS as a plan for decisions regarding your wealth. It states your risk tolerance, time horizon, and other facts about your objectives. You can also document your investment philosophy, lay out the process to rely on to evaluate investment opportunities, and list the constraints to consistently apply to your investment decisions.

Knowing what you want is just as important as knowing what you don't. Writing an IPS will play a significant role in your financial well-being by maintaining your objectives in a practical way. Your IPS governs what you will do and will not do in the future so that when a transactional decision arises, and your biases tempt you to act, following your IPS will help you avoid regrettable biases.

Now is an ideal time to establish guidelines for decisions, while you have your goals and objectives top of mind. Review your answers to the eight activities in Chapter 4 to identify areas of vulnerability, values, and risk tolerance before you proceed. Also, remember that you can tailor the IPS worksheet below to suit your objectives. Feel free to add or change any areas that suit you.

YOUR PERSONAL INVESTMENT POLICY STATEMENT

Name:	Date:

Personal Economic Values:
Insert your personal mission statement from Chapter 4. This defines your values and drives your future investment goals and decisions.

Background:
In this section, list your age, income, and current assets by type. Describe your investment experience. This is a snapshot of where you are now. If you're an insider or hold a controlling interest of any publicly traded companies, make a note of them to share with the investment professionals you work with.

Investment Objectives:
Review Chapter 4, Step 2, *How do you see yourself?* What you want to earn, do, and acquire? From that list, consider your savings strategies related to these goals. Decide when and how you will generate and save the assets needed to attain these goals. For example, if you want to retire in seven years, determine the amount of money you'll need to save and the return you'll require in order to understand the type of investment you'll need to hold to reach those objectives.

Describe what you need to achieve with your savings and investments to arrive at each of your goals. You may also want to include your
expected target return. A financial planner or investment professional
can help project these figures and other calculations, and guide you
through this process.

Complete any of the suggested statements below or add some
of your own.

I will need $_____ in _____ years for _____.
I expect to earn an average of ___% return each year.
I seek to outperform a benchmark of __% of the Canadian bond index
   and __% each of the Canadian and US stock markets (or some other
   benchmark).
When I retire in _____ years, I'll need income of $_____ after-
   tax, in today's dollars.
I want to grow my investments at the expense of volatility over a full
   market cycle.
I prefer to have my investments grow steadily with lower highs and
   higher lows.

Time Horizon:
From Chapter 4, Step 2, *How do you see yourself?* establish the timeline
for each of your financial objectives. Are there activities and experiences that you'll need to fund at specific dates? When will you retire,
or go to school (or send your children/grandchildren to school), or
otherwise need to use your savings? Are you a long-term investor, or
do you only have a few years?

By understanding your time horizon for investing, you can determine
what types of investments are most suitable. If you need a large amount
of your savings in a short period of time, it may be too risky to invest in
volatile investments, but if you can wait several years, investing in more
volatile investments provide much healthier returns. Similarly, you can
arrange investments that mature on a specific date to align with necessary
withdrawals, or to stagger so that they have a diversity of maturities. Below
are a few suggestions to identify your specific investment time frames.

I do not expect to withdraw funds from my savings for at least _____ years.

I can make investments that require a time horizon of _____.

I must keep __% of my portfolio available in investments that are accessible.

Risk Tolerance:

In Chapter 4, Step 5, you described what risk means to you and what you're prepared to tolerate. Recall from Chapter 2 that risk tolerance can change depending on your recent and other past financial experiences. Establishing your overriding risk tolerance helps to remind you of your long-range views, rather than your changing feelings and biases when volatility increases, or after substantial wins or losses.

Add your risk tolerance statement to your IPS. Include your comfort or discomfort with volatility. Describe what you will and will not tolerate, and what causes you to lose sleep, or which types of situations may influence you to exit your investment strategy at the wrong time. You may want to list any specific issues that concern you.

I'd describe my tolerance for risk as_____.

I can withstand market volatility through a full market cycle of _____.

I worry most about _____.

I'm generally not concerned about _____.

Investment Strategy:

From Chapter 4, Step 4, review your beliefs about money, and identify those that relate to how you would like to invest in the future. In this section of your IPS, describe your investment strategy as a philosophy. The purpose of this section is to provide a summary of how you want your investments to perform and what you will specifically do to achieve that result.

Describe aspects of your general approach, such as whether you will focus on value-based investments, or whether you prefer momentum and growth strategies. Alternatively, you may want to select and hold low-cost, broad-market exchange-traded funds (ETFs) in a passive investment approach. Or, you may have something completely different in mind, such as investing in environmentally sensitive or socially minded investments. You can also include your desire to maintain or avoid leverage. Any explanation of how you want to grow your wealth is suitable to include. You can even describe the reasons for your approach since this will make it easier to stick to your methods in the future if you become tempted by an alternative.

The following sections will provide helpful descriptions of several investment strategies. Once you have read these, you may want to update your IPS to incorporate or amend your strategy.

You may decide to hire a professional manager to take the reins. In this case, this section will help you select a professional advisor who uses a similar approach.

Asset Allocation:

The quantity that you allocate to various asset classes is determined by several factors, including the following:

- the pace at which you want your investments to grow;
- the amount of time that you can allow your investments to oscillate in the market;
- your willingness and capacity to accept volatility;
- the amount of cash you want to keep available;
- and when you'll need to draw on your savings.

Below, you can use the table to outline the minimum, maximum and target amounts of each asset class to maintain. For example, you may feel that it is prudent to keep 10% of your investible assets in cash, or you may feel that holding cash is a wasted opportunity. You can set those constraints below.

Asset	Minimum	Maximum	Target
Cash	%	%	%
Fixed Income (Bonds)	%	%	%
Canadian Equities	%	%	%

Asset	Minimum	Maximum	Target
US Equities	%	%	%
Other	%	%	%

Permitted Securities and Decision-Making:

By placing specific security constraints and decision-making processes on your IPS, you can navigate pitfalls and avoid the regret that comes with investing outside of your comfort zone. You may decide to restrict certain companies or sectors, such as oil and gas producers, or limit your investments to only large liquid companies by setting the minimum market capitalization to $1 billion or more. You may also decide to add guidelines that restrict investments in high-risk options to a maximum percentage of your holdings. Use this section to specify any constraints, limitations, and decisions that you want to avoid. The following phrases are only examples to get you started. Be as precise as you feel will benefit you.

- I only want to hold investments that _____.
- I will invest solely in opportunities that make me feel _____.
- All bonds will be rated a minimum of _____ credit rating.
- I will limit holdings in one issuer to a maximum of _____%.
- Derivatives may be used to _____ and will not exceed _____% of my portfolio.
- I will only invest in options with low/medium/high price variability measured by a beta of ___ or lower.
- I will not average-down on investments that drop in value.

Portfolio Monitoring and Rebalancing Frequency:

Earlier in this chapter, we introduced issues that arise when investors check their investments too often. Here is an opportunity to reduce your anxiety and limit the impact of frequent trading by planning to rebalance and review your investments on a schedule. For example, you may decide that your portfolio should be reset to your asset allocation every three months – this is called quarterly *tactical asset allocation*.

Or, if you use managed funds or ETFs, you may prefer to address it once a year.

If your investments are managed professionally, the need to review your investments is significantly reduced, assuming that the professional manages all ongoing decisions. In any event, you can decide the frequency that is suitable for your situation.

- Generally, I intend to hold onto positions for at least _____.
- I am targeting _____% turnover per year.
- I will review my investments no more than _____.

Once you've completed each of the sections of your IPS, save it where it is easily accessible for reference, and refer to it often.

I Knew-It-All-the-Time

"I had a feeling that Donald Trump would win the 2016 election!"
                                                    A Conservative Voter

After an event takes place, the outcome may almost seem obvious. In retrospect, certain signs will appear to be predictive of the ultimate outcome while contradicting facts easily fade away as irrelevant. You may even be inclined to think that if you had recognized the signs, you could have seized the opportunity. If only you had been able to act!

Hindsight bias causes memory distortion and regret. These feelings of clairvoyance may also lead to overconfidence in your ability to predict future events, since you feel so close to having predicted the past. Believing that you could have predicted a market correction, after it happened, will make you feel significant disappointment. However, feeling that you may be able to detect these circumstances the next time they arise can influence you to be jumpy as market values rise and fall. Sometimes, it may also drive you to withdraw from the market in anticipation of a significant price change, only to miss out on investment gains when the decline doesn't materialize.

Regardless of your emotional sensitivity, stock prices rise significantly more often than they fall. In any event, these dangerous beliefs can not only keep you on the sidelines instead of remaining invested, they also induce you to suddenly shorten your investment horizon when your original plan was a 5- to 10-year outlook. If you pull out of the market after a year or two, when your plan is to invest for decades, you'll inadvertently increase your risk of underperformance or even permanent loss of capital. Markets are unpredictable, but over the long-term, they generally trend higher. If investment market declines were predictable, no investor would buy securities above the lowest value that the market realizes after a decline.

If you need to change your investment strategy, the best time is when investment markets are calm and you have no urgency to do so. Your IPS is the ideal place to establish your investment time-horizon as a written policy. Then, it's ideal to prudently tether your plans to that timeline without regard for emotion or bias. Perhaps you have many years before you plan to retire, or you are only three years away from buying a piece of property. Whatever your horizon is, set it in writing and stick to it.

> *"I knew that China would recover faster than the US; I should never have sold my shares of Alibaba."*
>
> Stock Broker in Winnipeg

There is nothing as undermining as hindsight bias when it comes to well-intentioned financial decisions. The *could have, should have, would have* mental chatter destroys confidence faster than the Tasmanian Devil can rip apart a red-checkered picnic table.

Simply writing the basis of your investment decision provides a higher level of accountability that doesn't exist when you rely on gut instinct. It slows down the decision process, and gives you a chance to evaluate your choice more effectively. Writing down your reasons makes you stop and think about the decision at hand in a more calculated way. When you can slow down your decision process, you can account for your longer-term goals.

Whether you manage your investments or have a professional advisor, it's helpful to list criteria on which you plan to base your decisions in your IPS. For example, you may want to only hold investments with specific characteristics, such as dividend payors or those with low volatility (beta). You may remind yourself that selling suitable investments when the entire market drops isn't part of your strategy, regardless of how you may feel during periods of volatility. You may also point out that speculating isn't a suitable strategy to reach your goals – despite how beguiling a speculative investment may sound. Your beliefs about money in Step 4 will be helpful to establish what investments are suitable to you and which are not.

Regardless of what you include in your IPS, keep your written constraints simple to make it useful. The more complicated they are, the less likely you'll adopt them.

Cut Your Losses

"I'm going to average-down on this position so that I can recoup the money that I've lost."

A Biased Investor

The idea of *averaging down* is to buy more shares of the stock that you already own at a lower price. The goal with averaging down is to reduce your overall average cost. Buying more shares may lower your overall cost on the entire number of shares that you own, but it will never reduce your cost to the current price. That's impossible.

The argument for the strategy is that since the investment traded at higher prices in the past (since you bought them at that price), buying some more shares cheaper will lessen the amount the shares have to climb to break even. This faulty thinking is similar to the break-even effect from Chapter 2. If you feel that the investment is really an ideal strategy and everyone else is wrong, then it makes sense to buy more shares. But if you are seeking to regain an earlier loss, all you've really accomplished is investing more money in something that has already dropped in value. Throwing good money after bad has the added rub of owning more of an investment than you intended. Given that it has already dropped in value, you may not be very pleased with those prospects. Thanks to anchoring, when the earlier price was higher, you will be tempted to believe that the asset can return to that price-level, even without economic evidence to support such a conclusion.

The natural tendency to let nonrecoverable losses motivate you is compelling. If you've ever attended an event reluctantly, but only because you already paid for a ticket, you've experienced sunk-cost bias. When something is no longer relevant to your future, we should let go of the past expense or loss. Yet, in many situations, that is difficult. You are predisposed to continue with an investment strategy when you've already invested a meaningful amount of money into it, even when adding more money doesn't make sense. Abandoning the spent money produces feelings of loss, guilt, or regret, which we solve by throwing good money after bad.

It doesn't matter what you paid for an investment or how much you've already put on the line. If it no longer meets the criteria in your IPS, sell it. When you decide to invest in something that you already own, ensure that it meets the muster of a brand-new investment opportunity. Compare each investment – even ones that you already own – with all other opportunities before committing new money. This is a key addition to your investment decision criteria to add to your IPS.

Trees Don't Reach the Sky

> *"The market keeps dropping. It feels like it is bottomless. I should liquidate my investments before I lose everything!"*
>
> A Panicked Investor

> *"This cloud-storage stock is on a tear since it's a new issue. I'm definitely going to ride this one all the way up!"*
>
> Overheard at the Office

The **recency effect** crowds out past lessons with the urgency of the here and now. It's easy to get caught up in the day-to-day rhythms of news stories, risks, and current capital market patterns. You'll be pulled to think that what is happening now will likely keep happening into the future, or at the very least, over the next while. After all, it's relevant.

The following table shows the average rise of a variety of asset classes between 1900 and 2015. These returns are adjusted by the average inflation rate over the 115-year time frame.

Real Returns of Asset Classes (Adjusted by the Rate of Inflation)

Canadian stocks 7%	US stocks 8.3%	Canadian bonds 2.8%
US bonds 2.5%	US Treasury bills 1%	US houses 0.5%
Art 3%	Stamps 3.5%	Wine 6.7%
Violins 5.7%	Gold 1.8%	Silver 2.4%
Diamonds 1%		

(Chambers & Dimson 2017)

You may feel uncomfortable with the accuracy of this data if you've had a substantially different recent experience from these long-run returns. You may be tempted to claim that times have changed or that these long-term results don't represent prevailing opportunities. **Recency bias** persuades you to view your prospects relative to current information instead of taking a longer historical view.

This table of long-term averages, adjusted for inflation, provide a sound gauge to detect whether prevailing data is sustainable or temporary. Relying on a narrow view of history to predict the future is dangerous. Evaluate your expectations with data from long-term trends, rather than swinging from last year's best performing fencepost to the next.

For example, contemporary investors sometimes overestimate real estate returns as a superior asset class based on recent experiences, even though equities have plainly outperformed real estate over a long time horizon. That doesn't mean that there can't be short periods when equities underperform. Still, the price appreciation of real estate has returned even less than bonds, in aggregate.

Despite the evidence of price performance, there are reasons real estate may still appear to grow faster than other asset classes. First, for most of us, real estate represents the largest investment we will make in our lifetimes. Frankly, the numbers are big. Earning 2.5% per year for 10 years on a $1,000,000 property gives you a $280,084 profit. Compare that to a $50,000 stock portfolio at 8.3% over the same period. You only have $50,000 invested, yet it produces $110,982. Families are inclined to invest substantially more in a home than in a stock portfolio. You can't live in your investments!

Nevertheless, consider if you sold your home in 2021 for $1.65 million, having bought it in 2002 for $560,000. You may be tempted to think that you earned a cool million-dollar profit. Yet, it is only a compound return of 5.85%. If you had invested $560,000 in the stock market for two decades, your gain would have been even higher.

Second, due to the size of real estate transactions, most people leverage their investment. Most families need a mortgage to buy a house. Suppose you invest 25% of your funds to a million-dollar investment, while borrowing the rest. In that case, your $250,000 investment literally doubles in 10 years since the $1,000,000 value is what is appreciating at 2.5%. If you invest the same $250,000 in a stock portfolio, borrowing $750,000 for a total $1 million investment, your returns would be equally enhanced.

Real estate is not only an investment. It also provides the added benefit of reducing your rent costs since you can live in the house you bought. If you took your down payment and invested it in the stock market, you'd still need somewhere to call home. Another benefit of investing in your primary home in Canada is that there is no tax on the appreciation of your primary residence, and in the US, mortgage interest costs are often tax deductible. These are critical tax advantages.

The disadvantage is that real estate is less liquid than publicly traded stocks, bonds, and ETFs. Nevertheless, this illiquidity may be advantageous to combat bias. Unless you're thinking of selling, you will likely only consider the value of your home once a year when you receive the government assessment for property tax calculations. As discussed earlier in this chapter, checking your investments too often creates emotional responses that can induce you to trade your assets at the wrong time. Real estate's natural illiquidity forces you to forget about the day-to-day changes in the value of your home. Moreover, when your annual assessed value drops, you aren't likely to suddenly list your house for sale in fear that the value will continue to slide. You must live somewhere, and other property values have likely also dropped, so there's no point in selling when all prices are lower.

It is sobering to see the long-run returns of various asset classes, recognizing that assets typically rise more than they fall. It's easy to be lured to adopt preferences for trading patterns and asset classes; however, recalibrating will provide a more objective viewpoint on the best opportunities for you to invest.

In the Absence of Research

"I always get excellent service and they produce high-quality product. This stock is a good investment!"

A Biased Investor

"I'll never buy preferred shares again. They do nothing but lose money!"
An Unfortunate Prospective Client

A conventional approach to investing is to rely on your past experiences and to consider the merits of future investments based on past examples or similar options. However, as illustrated in Chapter 1, we tend to overestimate the usefulness of applying these proxies and rules of thumb.

We tend to think that things are more similar than they are. We draw inferences from similar examples or past experiences. For example, it's easy to jump to conclusions about an investment by what it is called. Or, you may think that if a company produces quality products, they will make a good investment. You aren't the only one who turns to **representativeness** to evaluate the merits of a choice under time constraints. We all do and it's natural to use rules of thumb. The danger is when you believe that the comparison is closer than it really is.

Investment regulators require managed investments to publish the disclaimer that past results are not an indication of future returns. Despite these warnings, the most common question that I hear from prospective clients is, "What was the performance of the portfolio last year?" We inherently believe that past returns can tell us about the future returns, but past returns are a better indication of outperformance or underperformance, and not about performance in general. Investments that outperform the benchmark during certain market conditions tend to underperform at other times – as expected.

When selecting an investment professional or an ETF, four key questions are critical:

1. What are the strategy's investment processes and constraints?
2. What is the relative performance compared to the benchmark, and what qualities are that performance attributed to?
3. How much risk does the strategy take in excess of the benchmark to achieve returns?
4. How does the proposed investment process avoid behavioral biases?

Note that none of these questions was about the returns they produced last year. An investment strategy that is true to its methods will typically underperform from time to time. It is this consistency that benefits an investor with the long-term views.

Momentum investing is the general process of following market trends. Momentum strategies do well during times of growth, but retreat more aggressively when markets drop because trend followers often push prices beyond the fundamental values of the underlying investment. Nevertheless, this approach can be quite profitable when the trend is rising.

In contrast, value investing is when an investor buys securities that are underappreciated, at prices below their fundamental value. Investors hold the position – sometimes for extended periods – waiting for them to appreciate. Value strategies work over the long run because there are less dramatic drops in value when markets retreat because the securities are already undervalued. The rise of these securities' prices doesn't need to be as dramatic as that of a momentum investment to produce solid long-term performance because there are fewer momentous losses.

Imagine what would happen if you were to switch from a momentum strategy after a big drop and into a value strategy that appears more stable, at the wrong time. You might be tempted to move back to the momentum strategy when the price changes in the value strategy isn't rising as quickly. In both cases, you would lose out on the benefits of both strategies.

Moreover, asset classes that dramatically rise are more likely to cool-off at or below their long-term averages because of the extreme increase. Using short time frames as your rule of thumb for big winners is dangerous. Yet, the fear of missing out on future returns can impel you to buy at the wrong time.

Everyone is prone to the influences of representativeness. However, studies have shown that training can markedly reduce its impact on decisions.[9] This is a decent reason to rely on the expertise of an advisor. Understanding the way that an investment is expected to behave during an investment cycle or under various conditions can mean the difference between bailing on a quality strategy that is doing what it should be doing, and one that isn't. Also, building a portfolio of investments that work well together is more reliable with necessary time invested to research each option – a resource not always readily available to individual investors. Moreover, relative performance and correlation analysis over long periods is a critical evaluation tool that can be dismantled by an investor's natural biases. Therefore, hiring a professional who operates at arm's length can provide a valuable firewall between you and your wealth.

Whether you rely on professional advice or not, defining your objectives and limitations in a written document is invaluable. Biases have a difficult time wielding power against a written reminder of your intentions. An IPS is for everyone.

Be Average

Roughly half of all investors enjoy above average returns. That's a mathematical fact. Furthermore, investment portfolios produce average returns more than any other value. I want to pause for effect, and let that sink in.

Consider the broad stock market index as a proxy for the average return. After all, to claim that you've outperformed the market, you need to deliver excess returns above this benchmark. The S&P500® index represents the 500 largest public US companies. In Canada, the S&P/TSX® measures the largest 300. The net daily gain or loss of these indexes is the aggregate price change of each of the listed companies. The increase or decline of each stock price is weighted by the size of the company, so the larger the company, the more impact it will have on the index. As some stocks rise and others fall, the broad market index provides a good feel for the rise and fall of the overall economic growth.

The same theory about portfolio performance applies to other asset classes, too. Beating the relative index or benchmark means that you've chosen instruments producing excess returns. Investors with higher profits either correctly gauged the market or were lucky. Those who underperformed suffered poor choices, biased decisions, or fell victim to random chance. Or, they may have held too many positions or traded too many times. When you hold so many investments that your portfolio resembles the index too closely there is little opportunity to outperform due to impact of transaction costs. Frequent trading also increases the risk of underperformance due to a market timing exposure and the gap between buying and selling prices.

Even though most investors earn average returns and half under-perform, you are more likely to hear stories bragging about extraordinary profits that the contrary. Despite the significant number of people whose investments flounder, it's rare to catch a backyard-barbecuer droning on about his pitiful investment blunders. There's no joy in sharing a story of folly.

Sure enough, people are delighted to boast about trading boons while predictably sweeping failures under the carpet. If most people earn an average return, and only about half of investors outperform, it is likely that the backyard swank has skeletons in the closet, too. People's investment behavior is relatively consistent. Those who reap astonishing returns on one investment will likely host a bevy of other investments with similarly risky profiles. Exceptional returns often relate to exceptional risks, at least some of which won't pay off.

Losses are painful enough without broadcasting one's disappointment across the back lawn. Since a disproportionate number of the tales depict investment wins, when you hear one you can confidently assume that there is an equally ugly story that isn't told. So, there is no need to feel that you're missing out.

Also, consider the effect that price swings take on a high-risk portfolio. When a $100,000 investment declines 20%, you're left with $80,000. You'll need to earn 25% on the $80,000 left to regain the starting value. Meanwhile, a boring investment that only lost 10% has more money to work with. The remaining $90,000 will be reconstituted to $100,000 with only a 12.5% return. Dramatic volatility doesn't necessarily provide the best performing investment, even when the headline returns sound fantastic.

If you find yourself in the bottom half of investors who lag, you are not alone. Trying to make up for losses by increasing your risk rarely ends well. Instead of doubling down, consider a direct investment in an index that represents the broad market and leave it alone to do what it's meant to do. There are many low-cost ETFs available from a variety of issuers that replicate any index that you want to follow.

By investing in the entire market at a low cost, you eliminate the risk of underperformance. You'll also enjoy an added benefit of reducing your stress and freeing yourself from the labor of researching investment decisions. Put your feet up on the ottoman with a cup of steaming coffee between your hands, and congratulate yourself for outperforming half of all investors by being average. In this case, being average is excellent.

The Unbiased Habit Checklist

Below is a checklist of critical habits that you can adopt to manage your investments, negotiations, spending, saving, and other financial decisions more effectively:

1. *Discover your PEVs.* Invest a weekend to discover your personal economic values. Print your PEV statement and keep it where it will remind you of your underlying values at the most critical moments. Every year or two, take an afternoon or a weekend to review the eight steps in Chapter 4. Then, align your decisions with these objectives so that the cumulative effects of your choices lead you to your goals rather than making a series of event-driven transactions that may lead you astray. This process will also result in fewer decisions overall because each of your decisions will direct you to your goals. You'll also limit the negative effects of bias on your outcomes when you center your decisions on your PEVs.

2. *Keep an uncomplicated financial business plan by writing an investment policy statement.* Provide a copy to any professionals helping you reach your financial goals. Reread your IPS prior to your periodic investment review or whenever you make important investment decisions. Reviewing this document brings your constraints, objectives, and other essential guidelines top of mind when formulating decisions. This tool is also an excellent way to communicate with

professionals, aligning their advice with your goals, and for holding them accountable.

3. _Implement routines and strategic habits_. Knowing about bias is not enough to keep you from its influence.

4. _Don't take it personally_. Avoid the displeasure of feeling responsible for the outcomes from random events. Instead, focus on your long-term goals and disregard market gyrations. You'll be tempted to believe you see patterns in unexpected price changes. Market events are largely unpredictable, and hindsight bias leaves powerful feelings of regret. If you could have made a different choice with the information you had, you would have.

5. _Stop checking your investments_. Consider suppressing your monthly investment statements and stop watching investment news broadcasts so keenly. Instead, schedule an annual review of your assets to confirm transaction accuracy, adherence to your strategy, and track your goals and returns. If you are your investment manager, schedule your reviews in advance at a frequency that makes sense rather than attending to your decisions during dramatic or stressful financial events when emotion and bias are influential.

6. _Calculate the percentage – rather than a dollar amount – that your investments grow each year compared to a relevant benchmark_. Adjust your returns to account for your contributions, withdrawals, and fees. Relative returns help limit the psychological impact that anchoring and high water marks have over the satisfaction you feel about your investments. Also, a comparison to the broad investment market will demonstrate when your strategy is successful or whether you are one of the 50% of investors who can improve your performance by investing in a passive broad-market strategy instead.

7. _Record investment decisions where you can store and retrieve them_. Rereading past thoughtful decisions can limit the emotional influence of hindsight bias. The process of writing things down also promotes a higher accountability in your process and more thorough due diligence. Moreover, it's easier to detect when your initial investment criteria have changed when you can refer to your initial decision criteria, often informing when to exit a strategy or encouraging you to stick to your convictions.

8. _Document strategies and investments to limit or avoid altogether._ For example, you may decide not to invest more than 25% of your assets in companies that don't pay dividends. Or, you may prefer to avoid businesses in a particular industry or sector. You may decide not to speculate, hold volatile stocks below a minimum market capitalization (size). You may also wish to avoid certain investment schemes or well-meaning nonprofessional advice. Whatever your constraints are, record them in your IPS.

9. _Control your enthusiasm._ Whenever you make a financial decision, compile a list of reasons why you shouldn't make that choice. You will better calibrate your outlook by building a strong counterargument rooted in rigorous skepticism. You may be inclined to feel that it's a waste of time because your natural tendency is to seek supporting information, not generate counterarguments. This bias will motivate you to cut corners and can just as easily throw you under the bus.

10. _Define the conditions to invest in or exit an investment strategy in your IPS._ Only buy or hold securities that meet your criteria for investment. If an investment no longer meets your objectives, is no longer suitable, or when it meets your reasons to exit, sell it. Other than for calculating taxes, the price you paid for an investment is irrelevant. The adage to buy low and sell high is an oversimplification of the math behind making a profit, not advice.

    Also, selling investments that rise for the sole purpose of capturing a capital gain, or holding onto stocks that drop hoping they'll regain former a price, are not investment strategies. They are examples of bias at work.

11. _Begin a save-more-tomorrow investment plan._ Commit to increasing the amount you save annually or whenever your income rises. Similarly, increase your mortgage or loan payment by any amount each year. Each additional payment you make is directly applied to reducing the amount you owe. Automate these increases whenever possible.

12. _Save the big money._ The proportional money effect influences you to focus on small values when transactions are small and disregard these values as the transaction size increases, yet large transactions offer the best opportunity to keep more of your money.

13. *Use anchoring to your advantage in negotiations.* Offer the highest reasonable price that will entice a buyer to accept or counter your offer. As a buyer, anchor the seller to the lowest reasonable price to induce the seller to respond. The following counteroffer will provide information about their willingness to amend their price. With that information, offer your best and last price, and always be willing to walk away from the transaction if the price is not fair.

14. *Guard against an early settlement.* Patience pays off when the likelihood to receive full value is reasonable. It just feels more comfortable to create certainty. Figuring out the price of early settlement can be an effective way to evaluate what you're giving up to satisfy your fears.

15. *Convert time to money.* The sooner you start any savings plan, the sooner your money begins the doubling process, and the less capital you'll need to invest overall. Time is literally money. One way is to immediately participate in a company-sponsored investment plan when its available, even if you're unsure about your options. It is more critical to begin the program than to select the ideal investment. Another is to start a small contribution to your savings, even if you don't know your plan yet.

16. *Use technology to automate every aspect of your finances possible.* Preestablished decisions reduce bias and emotion in your choices. Reducing the number of choices you face limits the effects of bias and the stress of decision-making.

    For example, by establishing electronic contributions, your fear of volatility won't interrupt your well-devised savings plan. You can also schedule time to review your investments and financial affairs on a specific date. Program fixed expenses, various payments, and other asset transfers with your bank. Automate periodic rebalancing of your investments so that your assets are brought back into line as market prices shift. When complete automation is not possible, schedule a reminder, and for each task, include all instructions, guidelines, processes, contacts, and other helpful information to reduce impediments to completing the job.

17. *Avoid crowded trades.* Consensus hurts performance because those who trail early investors have less to gain. Despite the increase in confidence when following the crowd, doing so can increase your risk unnecessarily.

18. _Use mental accounts to your advantage_. Set aside funds for your fixed expenses and long-term goals in a separate account. Apply both regular income as well as windfalls to your fixed costs, long-term objectives, and non-tax-deductible debt. Similarly, apportion some of your regular income to personal enjoyment.

19. _If you're working with an advisor, share your PEV and IPS with them_. Have them provide insights into their strategy to manage your assets, their decision-making processes to limit bias, and the method to evaluate your results.

20. _Be average._ If your investment strategy isn't performing up to your expectations, consider investing in the broad market using low-cost ETFs instead. You'll eliminate your risk of underperformance and have the added benefit of reducing stress.

Chapter 6

What an Investment Advisor Can and Cannot Do

The Bottom Line

Hiring a professional advisor has essential advantages. Reducing trading spreads, avoiding administrative errors, and passing off the time-consuming work of research and security analysis are among the most obvious. Another is to intervene in behavioral biases and provide an emotion-firewall between events and your investing behavior. But implementing and maintaining your **personal economic values (PEVs)** is the most meaningful reason to hire an expert.

Nevertheless, despite conventional wisdom, there are certain aspects of investment advice that even a professional, surprisingly, cannot perform reliably.

Bull Markets and DIY

Do-it-yourselfers (DIY) can find helpful and inspiring online videos for everything from setting up a crib to installing a kitchen faucet.

Half-hour programming inspires everyday folks to renovate a run-down bungalow and flip it for profit, despite no formal training in construction or real estate sales.

The lessons of any DIY are to be prepared to make mistakes. Hopefully, small ones. Yet, sometimes those errors can cause more than a black thumbnail from haphazardly swinging a hammer. Investment mistakes can lead to financial setbacks that are more than just unfortunate.

For decades, the investment industry has offered discount brokerage and online self-administered investment accounts. These platforms usually gain popularity during economically stable times, when investing seems effortless and even mediocre stock selections are profitable. During times of prosperity, it's easy to be lured into a false sense of security. Outside of tax and financial planning strategies, it's times like these when paying for professional advice feels redundant.

During heydays, stocks with lofty forecasts are driven up by **herd mentality**, **confirmation bias**, and **overconfidence,** lulling investors into complacency. However, when volatility erupts, shareholders who aren't sure what to do next freeze like a deer caught in the headlights, immobilized by the angst of **loss aversion**. During extreme economic unpredictability, it is more than a little tempting to step out of the way and take a breather. "*I can always get in later once it calms down*" is a favorite reason to leave the investment arena altogether when you don't know how to proceed.

If that wasn't disheartening enough, the **disposition effect** then lures you to capture gains on stocks that have risen, while the **sunk-cost effect** and **anchoring** nag us to hold onto those that have dropped in value. Those investors who panic and sell during instability can end up holding onto cash too long due to influence brought on by the **status quo bias**. Fear and indecision can be paralyzing when you don't know what to do.

The **recency effect** keeps your mind focused on the risks you face even when recent market declines have already priced them into the market. Sometimes security prices become oversold relative to the risks at hand, creating an opportunity. Yet, it's easy to find yourself unwilling to get back into the ring when the punches are still flying. Still, you'll never win a fight for wealth by standing at the concession stand.

Investors are not emotionally built to buy low and sell high. That's when the DIY approach falls apart. Taking risks in the wrong place or at the wrong time, or reeling back too far and remaining uninvested too long can harm your financial success just as much as investing in poor choices that lose money. An emotional firewall and professional assurance that you'll reach your objectives is invaluable when it maintains the path to your goals.

Even professionals are subject to bias, but education, training, and time devoted to indoctrinating systematic processes improve a professional's opportunities to be more effective. Of course, all people are subject to their own set of skills. Professionals, however, have an added advantage when they employ structured processes and documentation to mitigate these effects. Typically, they have also gained sobriety through experience and benefit from an arm's length relationships with their clients. Also, training and practice in recurring scenarios build skill, access to costly resources, and dedication to the craft improves the research and execution processes.

Each onset of dramatic events comes with its own recipe. The news headlines before the wild market volatility between the peak of the stock market on February 24, 2020, and the depths of the trough to follow four weeks later, were not any more telling than on any other day that proceeded it. Not CNN, FOX News, nor the CBC deviated from the prevailing news trends to alert the public to the significant economic risks of a pandemic. For weeks after the city of Wuhan, Hubei, China, began their lockdown on 23 January 2020 – a month before the market turmoil in North America – the health concerns of the mounting pandemic were a world away. It's common to underreact and to believe that what is happening right now is likely to persist. Besides, other epidemics in recent history were contained, so the initial reaction was to not take this one seriously.

Surprisingly, no one was shaken by the World Health Organization's declaration of Covid-19 as a Public Health Emergency of International Concern on January 30, 2020. Instead, investors marched in lockstep herd mentality, buying stocks in unison, and pushing the market higher by 3.44% for three more weeks (Source: Refinitiv). North American media was busy mourning the death of basketball legend Kobe Bryant and his young daughter in a helicopter crash in the hills above Calabasas, California.

The chilling disintegration of market prices began without notice or fanfare. No one wanted to miss out on the possible returns ahead, leading to the next US presidential election. The sitting president had demonstrated his pro-business inclination and his preparedness to throw more crates on the economic bonfire. Investors anticipated that they had not seen the last cord of wood flung onto the heap to keep the flame burning. The low volatility leading up to the third week of February indicated a high level of comfort that the fiscal spending would continue.

Over the four weeks that followed the February peak, the S&P500® whipsawed through single daily losses accumulating to −71.3% and single daily gains of 49.6%. Volatility spiked by more than 400%. Finally, the US stock market, representing the world's largest economy, settled at a net loss of −33.5% at the bottom in the third week of March (Source: Refinitiv).

After the first week that stocks plummeted, investors who hit the panic button crystalized losses by selling on one of the days that the stock market dropped by an uneasy amount. In many cases, the losses were hefty. Those who hung on to their stomachs and investments recovered losses by summer's end. The US index rebounded enthusiastically as fiscal and monetary government agents around the world promised to support businesses and families against lost wages and profits. Losses in the broad market evaporated by the start of the school year. Investors who stood their ground or didn't pay any attention to the anxiety created by volatility reconstituted their retirement and other savings accounts.

Despite the recovery of prices, the media kept their audiences on high alert with agonizing reports of rising infection rates, hospitalizations, and mounting death counts. In the summer of 2020, #BlackLivesMatter protests and US political rallies ignored the Centers for Disease Control recommendations for social distancing, raising concerns among many health care workers that COVID-19 would spin out of control. In many cities, protests turned to anti-police riots, harming both large chain stores and small businesses. Sideliners could only watch and wait out the anticipated health and economic impacts. By autumn, the incumbent US president instilled doubt of a peaceful transition of power following the November 2 election. It was a startlingly unsettling year to invest.

Many investors clung with frayed nerves, watching in horror as new COVID-19 cases rose across the globe in those early months. The prophesized second wave of infections prompted a weary stance across a wide range of investment options. Countless investors held onto significant piles of cash, thinking that the market would drop back to the low values seen earlier that year. Those people on the sidelines missed the price recovery, despite feeling prudent for being conservative.

Three years hence, the emotional turmoil subsides, and we will recall personal tragedies and news highlights, and only the net returns or losses over the entire period. By then, hindsight bias, availability bias, and recency effect will have reframed the events. The investment experiences of 2020 will be reviewed with facts and performance numbers that measure the successes and errors in aggregate, and in the rearview mirror.

Those who stayed the course, investing their money into volatile securities, were not delusional. There were ample reasons to invest in unstable markets where fiscal policymakers were actively easing business rules and taxes. The Federal Reserve Board, Bank of Canada, and other monetary policy makers worldwide reduced lending rates and bought bonds to inflate their prices, driving interest rates lower. Government bodies around the world were concertedly committed to supporting shuttered businesses and unemployed citizens with cold hard cash, and a lot of it. They turned on the spigots of liquidity at a steady flow to save the world economies. Moreover, businesses that were already set up for online spending and produced cloud storage, chips, and mobile computing enjoyed the boon, even under the tenets of a significant economic downturn.

Despite the millions of people who were suddenly unemployed and sequestered in their homes for health and safety reasons, there were decent reasons to invest for the future. There was an expectation of tough times ahead, of course. Still, when government agents are resolved to keep the population financially solvent, that kind of economic impact is like Goliath wielding a sword.

Understanding the difference between facts and opinion takes the experience of a weathered seaman. Professional advisors parse through news and data to drill down to the key influences on the market ahead. Professionals don't necessarily receive better information than mainstream news in today's immediate and widespread access to the internet. However, it sometimes takes practice and education to separate reputable sources of information from unfounded pontificators. That can be a function of experience. Practice can also provide a thick skin and higher tolerance to emotional events.

Media is in the business of selling advertising. In jockeying for higher readership, media outlets need to format information to catch people's attention and gain a higher readership. Nothing draws people in as quickly as controversy. However, drama is what investors need to avoid. When media outlets fan the flames on a situation, education and experience helps to sort through the theater and find the turning points that drive economic markets.

It's tempting to manage your own investments due to high accessibility and reduced fees. However, despite best intentions, biases can meddle with your decisions and ultimately affect your returns. Relatively low portfolio management fees are well worth paying when they reduce the negative impact of bias on your investment success. Also, by outsourcing the administration and day-to-day investment decisions, you can reduce your overall stress and liberate your time.

If you're keen to manage your investments but lack the time to conduct research and ongoing management, it's worth considering the merits of passive investing over your time spent to adequately evaluate the investments you select. As discussed earlier, passive investing reduces your risks and produces consistent, average investment returns. Average returns beat the results of half the investing population, as long as you aren't tempted away from your strategy by the fear of missing out.

Is Passive Investing a Silver Bullet?

There are measurable reasons to hire an investment professional. Outperforming an index isn't typically one of them.

Every year, SPIVA® compiles data on the performance of actively managed investment funds. 91.84% of Canadian Equity funds underperformed the S&P/TSX® Composite in 2019. Extended periods are even worse. Over sequential five-year periods, 96% of funds fail to meet the index returns every calendar year. Longer studies confirm that the average actively managed mutual fund underperforms once fees are calculated, and even the best funds don't consistently outperform the market.[1]

The US has a significantly larger pool of publicly traded stocks and a relative number of investment managers to choose from compared to the Canadian market. Yet outperformance in Canada is almost as abysmal. Fewer than 20% of active managers outpaced the S&P500® index every calendar year for five years running. Moreover, S&P Global argues that the outperformance by the few who manage the feat is no more meaningful than random chance. Of the top half of best-performing funds in 2015, only 3.84% were able to maintain that status for five years running.[2] So why would anyone hire an investment manager, you may ask?

The comparison between active and passive mandates is not straightforward. Some strategies measure up better than others. For example, small- and medium-sized companies and dividend and income investment mandates outperform their related indexes more often than large, growth-oriented portfolios.

Also, when you invest in a strategy that beats one year and under-performs another, that doesn't mean that the returns over the entire five-year investment period are subpar. In fact, they may not have underperformed at all. If a portfolio lags in one of the five years, it might still outpace the index over the full five years. Also, a lower yet consistent return can outperform one that is more volatile. When an investment drops by 5%, you'll need to earn 5.26% to return to your original value since there are fewer dollars invested after the decline.

It used to be that actively managed funds were nearly the only option for investing in equities unless you wanted to pick stocks yourself. Today, however, index investing is easily accessible with exchange traded funds (ETFs) that replicate various markets and sectors for a meager cost. Some ETFs have embedded administration and trading fees that are as low as 0.02%. It's tough to complain about that successfully. ETF positions trade on the stock market, so commissions are still charged each time you buy or sell, but you can keep those costs to a minimum if you are planning to buy and hold or maintain an account at a low-cost discount broker.

The benefit of passive investing is that there is no risk of significant underperformance when the ETF you select replicates the index itself. Broad-market ETFs either invest in the index's constituents directly or use derivatives to mirror the index's price performance. Either way, these investments make a compelling alternative, as long as the index you've selected is what you're bargaining for. Some markets and strategies are more volatile than others, and passive investing isn't necessarily lacking volatility.

You'll still need the fortitude to stick with your plan when volatility erupts. Moreover, the fear of missing out (FOMO, pronounced fo-mo) might steer you away from your strategy by luring you to individual stocks. Despite the benefits of index investing, there are inherent risks of owning an index that every investor should understand. Also, you'll also need a little know-how to effectively trade an ETF on an exchange.

Several major indexes, such as the S&P500® and the S&P/TSX®, follow the largest publicly traded stocks in the US and Canada, respectively. Instead of each company holding an equal value in the index, both of these indexes weight each company according to its market capitalization. The market capitalization, or size of a company, is measured by the number of shares outstanding multiplied by the stock price. A portfolio of market-cap-weighted positions has the most exposure to the largest businesses and relatively little of the smallest ones.

When a large company's stock price rises or falls, it will disproportionately affect the index. As companies grow, the proportion of the index that they represent also increases. That isn't necessarily detrimental unless the price of a company's shares appreciates due to speculation rather than earnings growth. For example, you may feel content with Microsoft's stock when it trades at 40 times its earnings per share, but less easy with Shopify trading at 190 times the company's earnings per share.

Indexes are not particularly transparent, and investors may not be aware of concentration risk in a particular stock or sector. In 1999, the price of Canadian company Nortel Networks escalated during the technology bubble. This stock grew to represent roughly 30% of the Canadian stock market index. Just a couple of years later, the company was bankrupt. The Canadian stock index is not as diversified across the country's economic landscape as you may believe, either. The S&P/TSX®, for example, holds a concentration of banking and resource companies.

In the US, the most significant companies in the S&P500® are Microsoft Corp., Apple Inc., Amazon.com Inc., Meta Platforms Inc., and Alphabet Inc, making it much more influenced by technology companies.[3]

Passive investing refers to holding an entire index or sector as it is. ETFs provide easy access to both broad markets as well as a specialty markets in a one ticket investment solution. More recently, the introduction of Smart Beta versions of passive indexes enhances investors' ways to participate. Some ETFs, for example, provide index investing, but with a preference for certain types of securities or styles of investing. A tweak on the underlying index, if you will.

A beta of one denotes that the portfolio tracks the volatility of an index one-for-one. Therefore, an ETF that tracks a broad market index should generally have a beta measurement of one. Smart-Beta, however, is a rules-based investment approach meant to combine the efficiency of passive investing with a defined enhancement – a quasi-passive investment.

These aren't considered actively managed because the portfolio closely mirrors the underlying index, but has a strategic filter in place. For example, instead of sticking with the exact quantities of each stock in the S&P/TSX®, investors can buy an ETF holds all the constituents but at equal weights. While each stock in the index is still represented, companies with a small market capitalization affect the ETF's overall return as much as prominent ones do. In another example, a low-volatility ETF limits highly volatile companies whose share prices fluctuate to a higher degree.

The benefits of passive investing are its simplicity, low fees, and long-run returns. Although passive investing follows the undulating market swings, if you had invested with your eyes closed for the last 20 years, your investments would have risen with the tide. Instead, if you hang on each burp and giggle, the swings along the way are sometimes dislodging enough to make even the sturdiest investors lose their footing. Passive investing is subject to loss aversion, FOMO, and other emotional predispositions.

Despite exposure to some important biases, passive investing can make your life easier by reducing the time commitment for research, limiting trading and therefore trading errors, and reduce your risk of underperformance. If you can stomach the ups and downs – or limit the frequency you check your investments – passive investing and smart-beta investing can be ideal.

Intuition

The dangers of managing your own investments are rooted in the very reason you are motivated to do so: confidence and intuition.

There is no shortage of pseudo-experts spouting off unfounded yet confident opinions. Media personalities are only too keen to prognosticate the future to draw in audiences and attract advertisers. Online forums draw all sorts of individuals offering self-assured and sometimes conflicting investment advice. Even accredited professionals have been known to provide vague points of view and hapless estimations of what lies ahead.

In any event, the more confident the speaker is, the more credence we tend to give the message.

We put faith in people who speak with authority and tend to believe those who answer questions confidently. Yet, self-assuredness is rarely a reliable measure of accuracy. As many legal professionals have discovered from faulty eye-witness accounts, there is no correlation between conviction and truth. Intuition is one of those highly motivational sources. The question is, when is it reliable, and when is it not?

Intuition is when you suddenly become aware of something without knowing how you arrived at a conclusion. You walk into a parking lot and instinctively know that something is wrong. Or your brother opens the door and you immediately realize that it's your brother without thinking about it. It's the moment you know something, but you're not sure how you know it.

There is no shortage of fantastic stories of businesspeople and investors who relied on their intuition and reaped great success from the decisions that followed. Moreover, if instinct draws on your vast store of information and experiences, presumably, the more expertise you have to draw on, the better your intuition must be. So, when can you rely on professional intuition?

A professional can develop expertise and become an authority on aspects of their line of work. However, you don't need to be an expert to become a professional and not all professionals are experts.

Professional expertise is undoubtedly a robust skillset acquired through education, experience, or both. Bruce Lee once said, "I fear not the man who has practiced 10,000 kicks once, but I fear the man who has practiced one kick 10,000 times." The latter arguably develops expertise in that single kick. This is what athletes commonly refer to as muscle memory, a kind of instinctual execution of a physical movement.

Professionals may be proficient at certain aspects of their work, while they may be novices at other elements. Consider a lawyer who practices family law. They may be well-versed in the application of child support guidelines but know nothing about commercial real estate contracts. They may not even understand the nuances of child support guidelines in other territories where they are not licensed.

Skills can develop into reliable expertise when three conditions are met. The first is practice, practice, practice. Learning skills at a high level takes years of training and rehearsal. In his book *Blink*, Malcolm Gladwell popularized the idea that becoming an expert requires roughly 10,000 hours of deliberate practice to learn a skill. Deliberate practice is explicitly learning what the student has yet to master. It also implies that anyone can become an expert because anything can be learned.[4]

The second condition to develop expertise is that the training must provide immediate feedback. The value of repetition is wasted if you practice the wrong thing. Imagine playing a cello off-key in a world without sound. The value of feedback fortifies good results and punishes mistakes. Hissing strings that pierce your ears are not tolerated for long, even by a loving parent.

In finance, good and bad decisions are reinforced with profits and losses: live by the sword and die by the sword. Losses and gains are unmistakable, and market oscillations expose the validity of the trader's logic pretty quickly. Stock pickers suffer swift repercussions for poor choices and reassuring rewards for wins. We certainly want to replicate profitable trades that pay off, and feedback allows the practitioner to validate each decision's effectiveness.

Education provides a framework for evaluations and assessments, but practice hones the process to adapt to real-life experience. It can also improve the speed of execution as successful operations become increasingly automatic with repetition. The more times an action is reinforced with positive feedback, the more you rely on the process, and the more reflexive the decision process becomes.

The final condition required to develop expertise is a reliable environment. When the setting that a professional is mastering has regularity, the opportunity to become proficient is excellent. Repeatable scenarios can be learned with practice, including proficiencies in sports, music, or the moves to win a game of chess. The less variable the environment, the easier it is to master.

Both professionals and laypersons with a high level of expertise can develop what we typically refer to as intuition. It requires a significant amount of practice with reliable feedback in a sufficiently stable or repeatable environment. The third requirement is where the trouble starts for professionals in economics and the management of capital markets.

The stock market and the economy are influenced by such a massive number of factors that it would be impossible to attend to them all. People do not have the capacity to detect such a vast number of elements at any moment. It is already profoundly unlikely that any economic situation can reoccur in one's lifetime. The chance that you could predict it if it did is even more fantastic.

If professionals cannot develop categorical expertise in market timing or economic predictions, intuition on those subjects is therefore unreliable. Furthermore, if a financial expert is little more than statistically lucky at predicting the future despite education and experience, a layperson is even worse off.

The problem with intuition is that it comes with a healthy dose of confidence, even when there is no factual basis for the underlying conviction. Overconfidence waves a red flag; you can take steps to guard against falling under its spell with reframing (see Chapter 5), even when it's your own.

Intuition may be highly motivating. Regardless, it doesn't help in your investment prospects any more than chance. Relying on insights to pick lottery numbers or the next professional golf tournament winner is equally nefarious.

There are valid reasons to hire a professional. Intuition about the direction of the stock market isn't one of them. Even though intuition manifests along with a strong impression of its accuracy, a real expert understands the limits of their knowledge.

Beware. If an expert can't rely on instinct to predict market movements despite expertise and experience, neither can you.

Avoiding Hindsight Bias with Training

When portfolio performance falls below your expectations, it's impossible to avoid feelings of disappointment. **Hindsight bias** swiftly converts your original investment strategy and careful analysis into a view that focuses squarely on the poor results. After financial loss, the sensible reasons behind your decision are drowned out by regret and a painful nagging replay of what you should have done differently.

Consider, for example, an investment strategy that temporarily falls out of favor in the current market conditions. Value investing is a strategy to buy stocks that have been neglected by other investors. The share prices of value stocks are much lower compared to the company's earnings than their high-growth counterparts. In other words, these stocks offer a dollar's worth of corporate earnings at a lower price.

While research shows that value-investing is a successful strategy over the long-term, be prepared to feel disappointed for most of the journey. You will likely experience long bouts of underperformance during phases of strong economic growth. When popular companies' prices keep pushing higher, the news can perpetuate their popularity and drive prices higher still. This is nothing but annoying to value investors who may at some point question whether they adopted the right strategy.

After several years of underperformance, it is difficult to remember the prudence of the strategy. Year after year of comparatively lackluster results make even savvy investors second-guess their decision. Tested investment strategies, including value investing, can sometimes have long periods of poor results before the process pays off. Despite being a laggard, value investing has proven to be exceptionally successful! Just because a company is out of favor doesn't mean that it will always be forgotten. Eventually, quality companies with a relatively low cost catch investors' attention, and their prices can rise quickly to make up for lost time. When a market bubble pops and the prices of growth stocks deflate, investors often turn their attention to the underappreciated value stocks.

Hindsight bias gives us the feeling that we should have been able to foresee an outcome. We expect that a professional with education and experience should have predicted the economy or the market. However, as earlier argued, this is not much more likely than the odds of chance.

Information that could have predicted an event seems obvious only after the fact. Hindsight bias refocuses our attention from our thoughtful decision to invest, to the singular viewpoint of the resulting good or bad outcome. The next natural step is to find a scapegoat. Regardless of how methodical research may be, advice that results in loss ebbs away faith in the practitioner who delivered it. The outcome outweighs the process because people put more emphasis on looking backward after adverse events. Interestingly, positive results are typically scrutinized less vigorously.

Numbers and money are quantifiable. During long periods of low returns, it's natural to become critical. In frustration, some investors are attracted to the allure of little or no fees, justified by the savings of reduced fees. As an added benefit, moving your business to a discount investment strategy also punishes the decision maker that you want to blame for the market conditions.

Long-term averages of returns are an easy guidepost to use, like GPS directions to a new restaurant in a strange city. Inspired by a neighbors' tale of financial glory described over apple-stuffed pork tenderloin and one too many bottles of Sauvignon Blanc, a frustrated investor may resolve to move their portfolio to a discount broker. At least the management fees will be lower.

Our memories are short. It's difficult to remember that the returns of long-term equity result from prolonged periods of boring undulations that don't seem to go anywhere. It can be like a road meandering through the prairies, with nothing but the haze of a horizon ahead. Then unexpected episodes of sharp increases or declines, like hills and terrain, appear out of nowhere and startle us to pay attention again.

Investors aren't conveniently holding 100% cash at the lowest part of the market, poised and ready to invest at the very moment that the market turns up. Yet bull markets are measured from the lowest point of the last market drop to the eventual peak. Most people have had their RRSP invested for years, not beginning the day of the last stock market crash.

These measures tend to stoke the fire of loss aversion and herd mentality. If you hear that the market has risen 86% over the last five years, but your retirement plan has returned less, you'd be justifiably unhappy. Shouldn't your investments have kept pace, at least? But when the total return of the market since January is still down 5% despite the recent rebound, you'd probably be pretty happy with zero percent return and zero percent loss. That's outperforming the market.

The total gain beginning from the trough after a bear market drop isn't relevant. So, when the news reports that the bull market has returned a 40% rise in stock prices, that likely doesn't represent any investor's actual experience.

The average returns on investments over decades are a compilation of low growth, short bursts of high growth, and a few bear market pullbacks for good measure. Since these price swings are not predictable, if you miss either of the first two, you're unlikely to meet your objectives. Staying the course and remaining invested is the best way to achieve your goals.

The stock market reflects a wide variety of investors' opinions, all wanting to make more money than the next guy. It's nearly impossible to guess which direction it will head next, despite our desire to see patterns in price movements. When the crowds become unnerved and decide that it is time to sell, there isn't a dinner bell that rings as notice of the mass exodus.

Media reports don't seem to anticipate the tide of investment exuberance or withdrawal either, although they are happy to fuel its speculation. Neither are past earnings an indication of future growth or contraction. It's human biases that take hold to tip the scales from everybody onboarding to everyone jumping off.

It is impossible to predict the direction that the market will take next, except to say that economies generally grow over time, and people are generally optimistic. When the future is uncertain, the best approach is to align your investments with your PEVs and choose an advisor who supports your vision. It isn't an accident that people are drawn to like-minded people, including the professionals they hire.

When to Trust Expert Investment Advice

There are specific reasons to hire an expert investment professional. Intuition about how the economy or the course the capital markets will take is not one of them. Outperforming an index is also less productive than you may have hoped. Neither of those purposes will reliably advance your interests, but there are meaningful benefits to working with a professional investment advisor (IA) or portfolio manager (PM).

Investors often don't realize the money-saving efficiencies of working with a professional. Some professionals have negotiated foreign exchange rates with their firm's trading desk that reduce the spreads on large transactions. For example, suppose you are interested in exchanging US and Canadian cash. Your PM can combine your request with other foreign currency trades to increase the whole transaction's value. The larger the quantity being traded, the tighter the spreads between buying and selling currencies, and the better the exchange you'll pay.

Also, they can provide helpful conveniences. Contributing and deregistering investment contributions by phone with a professional who knows the sound of your voice makes life easy. The minutiae of financial tasks become uncomplicated when you don't need an appointment. The prospects of driving to an office, parking, and forgetting some of the paperwork at home is eliminated. Moreover, the advice on any resulting tax implications are helpful.

A professional will also identify the relative timing for contributions and withdrawals, and where best to allocate them. A PM can act as a fiduciary in representing your best interests.

You no longer need to be at the forefront of daily investment decisions. An investment professional determines the best assets to sell and which tax-shelter or nonregistered accounts to transact. Relying on professional advice for these functions eliminates your natural tendency to procrastinate about choices, reducing status quo bias.

An advisor can also help you move past the status quo bias by assisting you with financial options at work. When picking the funds for your money-purchase pension plan is unclear, your advisor can select funds to coordinate with your other investments. A financial advisor is often willing to help you understand the nuts and bolts of your financing terms, including leases, lines of credit, and mortgage options – which are all part of your overall financial plan.

Another advantage of working with an advisor is when they can cross securities among their other clients at the mid-market price. Imagine that you need to take $100,000 out of your investment account to help your son buy his first home. Your portfolio holds securities that trade at a large gap between the selling (bid) and buying (offer) prices. That is typical for securities that don't change hands often, or when transaction volumes are small. An offer of $11.78 is the best price for a buyer to fill their order. When the highest bid is $10.98, a seller who wants to liquidate their holdings cannot obtain a better price. However, crossing a position from one client to another can be executed in the middle of the two prices. Both the client buying the shares and the one selling benefit from a more favorable price than is available on the market.

Expert advice is not rooted in prognostication or confident opinion. It is, however, evident in transaction negotiations, investment management, and the skills required to execute trades efficiently. Those benefits can save you significant time and money, and are sound examples of when you can confidently trust expert advice.

Know What You Don't Know

The risk of judgment errors increases the further you operate outside of your expertise. And relying on seemingly practical advice can pose problems that aren't easily identified if you don't know what to look for.

General wisdom predicts that reducing expenses and taxes are always good strategies. However, as we have already seen, reducing fees at the cost of damaging investment errors is a false economy. Similarly, implementing strategies to save taxes without understanding the implications of the plan can be equally harmful. In some instances, paying the tax is much less expensive.

For example, tools such as joint ownership of assets and naming beneficiaries on registered investments are easily updated with the stroke of a pen, making the homespun estate planning alluring. The promise to pass assets directly to your beneficiaries and avoid the cost and time to probate a will through the courts sounds like a winning approach.

One example of such dubious advice is to add children to the title of your home so that if you decease, the house will pass to the child without being subject to probate. Suppose that mom lives in the home and adds her adult son on the title. The immediate problem with this plan is the fees for changing the title at the land title office. However, a more significant issue emerges when the son doesn't claim the home as his primary residence. In that case, capital gains accrue on his half of the house value, since the exclusion to capital gains is only granted to your primary home. He will owe taxes on his part of the increased property value, which will be owed to the Canada Revenue Agency when the house is sold or changes hands. If mom had left her residence solely in her name, it would have been entirely exempt from capital gains taxes.

More trouble will erupt with this scheme if the son runs into a liability issue. In that case, the house may be considered part of his assets and be called on to settle his debts. Suppose he is involved in an automobile accident and is underinsured. The other party may seek restitution, including claiming the home's value where mom lives. Similarly, a family lawyer may attach the home's value in a separation arrangement if the son dissolves his marriage. Ultimately, these risks are far greater than the comparatively meager cost of probate.

In another example, consider a man with a terminal illness who wanted to pass his estate to his two young nieces. He didn't have children of his own, so he arranged for his assets to transfer to a testamentary trust established in his will. They each stood to inherit several million dollars. The girls' father didn't want his children to receive such a large sum of money at a young age for fear they would make poor life choices, so the uncle detailed the trust to disperse half of the inheritance once the girls reach age 30 and the other at 35 years old.

The man then went to his office to speak to the human resources agent. There, he arranged for his nieces to be the sole beneficiaries of his pension plan and group insurance policy. He also met with his investment advisor and described his plans to gift his assets to the two girls. She added them as beneficiaries on his retirement accounts, which happened to be where the majority of his financial assets resided. He still needed his house and car for the time being, so he resigned himself to letting those assets go through probate.

Since the insurance policy and other registered plans each named the girls as beneficiaries, those funds were paid directly to his nieces when he died, thus thwarting their father's wishes to delay giving them so much money. The assets were not probated by the will, and therefore were never directed into the testamentary trust.

That wasn't the end of the calamity. As the executor, the brother was responsible for managing the house and car expenses until they could be sold. However, there were no liquid assets in the estate, since all of the investments and insurance were paid to the nieces. Additionally, the proceeds from the house sale were about all that was left in the estate to be directed to the testamentary trust. Nevertheless, the cost to administer the tax filings and manage the trust was ongoing for several years to come.

Coffee shop advice is as valuable as the napkin it's written on. A personalized financial plan with a professional advisor can save you far more than it will cost by avoiding destructive misinformation and over-simplified remedies. The roadblocks that lie ahead are not often easily identified unless you have experience or training to see them. Markets and economics may not offer sufficient reliability to be anything more than a practice. Financial planning, however, is unmistakably a professional area of expertise.

When selecting the type of professional advice that aligns with your needs, consider the specialties of various accreditations. For example, a financial planning expert provides expertise in the nuances of managing various aspects of private wealth planning. In contrast, a Chartered Financial Analyst (CFA) has a deep understanding of asset valuation and portfolio management. In addition, some professionals carry multiple designations and expertise.

Regardless of educational specialization, structured investment experience over full market cycles and across various market conditions cultivate a robust understanding of how investments can react under certain circumstances. For example, the price of preferred shares is more significantly affected by interest rates than by the company's earnings because it acts somewhat like a long-duration bond and a newer company with exponential earnings growth is likely to be more volatile than a mature one. Also, professionals can develop expertise to analyze a specific investment style and how market conditions can impact such a strategy. These areas of expertise are instrumental in selecting suitable securities that align with specific levels of risk tolerance and meet particular investment objectives.

Investment expertise is reliable for repeatable experiences in a relatively stable environment. Even an economist can provide insight into aspects of foreign exchange or understand the implications of something that has occurred. The key to avoiding pitfalls is to understand the bounds of expertise in general. It will always benefit you to understand your limits too, and the limits of the people you rely on.

Bias Resistance

Professionals and experts are not immune to the impact of most biases, including anchoring. You'll recall the experiment from Chapter 1, in which real estate agents were influenced by the list price of a home for sale, even though they were adamant that it wasn't a factor in their objective analysis of the house value. Anchoring is an automatic response that seemingly cannot be overridden even by professionals and nonprofessionals alike, despite their best efforts.[5]

However, training and expertise can successfully reduce the impact of other biases. You'll also recall the Knetsch research, from Chapter 1, on the **endowment effect.** In that experiment, participants valued the coffee mug or chocolate bar once it was in their possession more highly than the other item of equal value.

Studies repeatedly demonstrate that the endowment effect exists in stock and securities trading, where investors appear to value the shares that they own more highly than those they don't. Sell orders are typically listed further from the current market price than buy orders. However, trading frequency and experience significantly reduce the impact of the endowment effect – a benefit of practice and reliable feedback.

Investors can also reduce or eliminate the endowment effect by relying on an investment advisor for trading decisions. The endowment effect is induced by the anticipation of regret. You tend to feel less or no regret when you can share investment responsibility with others, such as your professional advisor.[6]

Professionals' training and experience carry advantages beyond limiting the forces of bias. Diligent professionals can dedicate time and resources and implementing strategies to avoid bias that aren't practical for people who aren't required to address investment decisions as frequently. Extensive note taking and documentation of market changes and client discussions, for example, are common practice in the investment industry. These habits reduce the regret of hindsight bias, the risks of overconfidence and overtrading, and the enticement of framing, to name a few.

Other strategies that investment professionals can implement include investment decision tracking, documentation of security selection, and instituting a structured sell discipline. Also, the Investment Industry and Regulatory Organization of Canada (IIROC) as well as the Securities and Exchange Commission (SEC) require extensive charting notes related to each client meeting and investment decision. Under the Canadian Client Focused Reforms of 2022, investment professionals are required to Know-Your-Product (KYP), by demonstrating an understanding of the terms, features, risks, and potential returns of each security, transaction, and trading strategy. They are also responsible for documenting how recommendations and transactions can assist each client in achieving their investment objectives, and how market volatility could affect potential returns.

Furthermore, professionals must display evidence of having reviewed alternative investments in the process of selection. When executed consistently, these strategies produce more predictable outcomes for clients by limiting the calamity of second-guessing investment decisions, or even worse, overconfidence. The increased attention to research details has obvious benefits for thwarting a number of natural biases. The time required by these rigors is difficult for individual investors to match – they generally have limited time to devote to such processes.

Portfolio Abandonment

If the amount of anguish you experience due to volatility and loss aversion is correlated to the number of times you review your portfolio, you can benefit from hiring a professional to intervene here, too.

Anecdotally, investors who manage their own investments are most dramatically affected by biases and heuristics. Even clients who accept the final say in each investment decision that their advisor recommends suffer more emotional responses than those who hire a trusted discretionary investment manager. It stands to reason. If you're ultimately to blame for each investment error, the success of each decision weighs more heavily on your conscience.

In one case, a prospective client argued that he prefers to be responsible for mistakes in his portfolio rather than to have a professional slip up. I'm confident that isn't true. He may have meant that he doesn't want to pay a professional to make mistakes when he is quite capable of making them himself. At least he'd be saving on the fees. This assumes that the professional will make the same missteps that the investor was making, of course, which we hope a professional would avoid.

Unfortunately, with the help of hindsight bias, even an educated investment decision can appear to be a blunder, despite who makes it or the quality of the decision process. The real underlying question about whether to pay for professional advice or not is whether an advisor can add value equal to or greater than the fees that they charge. Of course, the value of advice is measured in returns as much as it is in peace of mind, and other ancillary services and benefits that come with the program, such as financial planning.

Recently, I met with a fellow who was referred to me by an existing client. Each time we met, I noted how meticulously he dressed. After gaining his trust, he finally provided his investment statement to review. The pages that he scanned to my office listed some common shares, including Amazon.com, Inc. (AMZN), Apple Inc. (AAPL), and several other securities – mostly oil and gas companies – that had dropped in value. There was also a surprising $280,000 held in cash.

His portfolio had not been touched in quite some time, other than the recent purchases of AMZN and AAPL, for which he was only too quick to claim responsibility. They had been a bright spot on the statement.

There was little diversification and probably low returns for a long time, which he lamented over in a swath of hindsight bias. He said that he had given up on this account and didn't pay much attention to it anymore. He planned to sit on the shares that had declined until they returned to their original purchase price (loss aversion, sunk-cost bias, status quo, disposition effect). Then he planned to get out. He was anchored to the initial prices that he paid for each of the securities.

I recommended that he align his investment portfolio to opportunities that provided better prospects in a more diversified approach. However, he couldn't stomach the transaction. Selling the shares at a loss and buying different investments meant that he could lose money on the new ventures just as easily as he lost them on the last set. It was reasoning rooted in not understanding the investments that he was holding or the benefits of research and diversification. Loss aversion was preventing him from making a logical investment decision to sell securities that no longer served his objectives, and each discussion ended with the same conclusion.

He also struggled with the thought of paying portfolio management fees without first knowing whether his investment performance warranted the cost. He was focused on the value of professional portfolio management in terms of how it could produce additional returns to pay for the advice. However, if nothing else, it was clear that he would have benefitted significantly from releasing himself from the investment decisions that plagued him.

His accountant favored the plan to engage a professional and as he pointed out, the portfolio management fees are tax-deductible. However, even the advice of two experts was not enough to dislodge the investor from the status quo bias. The pain of loss aversion in his case was so intense that he was immobilized from improving his strategy to meet his objectives and values. And in the process, he would have reduced the related stress and anxiety generated every time he discussed this account.

There are many reasons why our interests fall to the bottom of our to-do lists. Even financial professionals have been known to neglect their investments. The reasons for doing so aren't always because we become too busy with other aspects of life. Many times, looking at assets that are up or down from where you purchased the securities generates uncomfortable emotions. It's easier to make an excuse and claim that it isn't as crucial as other investments or other parts of your life.

Of course, this money is as vital as other money. A natural deferral to **mental accounting** segregates suitable investments from bad ones. It is much more pleasurable to spend time and energy on the assets that make you feel profitable than those that generate negative effects. If your stock portfolio is suffering, it's a natural tendency to let it continue to languish, and neglect future decisions.

If dealing with these investments causes too much angst, hiring a professional to act as an emotional firewall could set things straight. Not only can they move you beyond the status quo and portfolio abandonment, but they can also lend support, advice, guidance, and advocacy to all aspects of your financial well-being. When you aren't sure where the ball is, hire a coach on the third baseline to signal if you should round the turn and come into home plate or stay on the base you're on.

Chapter 7

Can Money Buy Happiness?

M ost people report that if they could change one thing in
their life to increase their happiness, it would be to have
more money.

The torrid relationship between money and happiness is longstanding
and well documented. Yet, for most of us, blindly following the widely
held assumption that money buys happiness hasn't led to long-lasting happiness at all. There are plenty of wealthy people who are miserable, and
just as many examples of very happy folks with little money.

The details provided in earlier chapters delve into the common issues
that plague us in our pursuit of financial security, and ultimately, happiness. You've discovered many of the biases that affect your interpretation
of the world and how bias complicates financial decisions. You've read
about how and when bias undermines your best intentions to control risk.
And, you've learned how, unwittingly, you work to believe that you are
right, despite financial damages.

If we are all in the pursuit of happiness, and if financial security will get
us there, why are we each seemingly built to undermine our best efforts?

Can money truly buy happiness, or is something else at work?

185

Happiness, Work, and Retirement

Imagine that you are looking for work. You finally receive an offer for an ideal position at a top-rated firm. When the excitement subsides, concern settles in. They are offering you less than you made at your last position and you know how difficult it is to earn a raise once the bar is set.

You made more money at the interim position in the university co-op program last summer, or wherever you worked historically. The offer just presented is comparatively insulting, you decide. It feels like you're going backward instead of getting ahead.

Using the past as a guide isn't a bad idea. These yardsticks to assess the value of contracts are naturally based on your capabilities, aptitude, and the employment market, unless they prevent you from making a sound decision for the future. However, anchoring to the higher past wage has a cost. The old job doesn't exist anymore, yet, it's still important information. It gives you a gauge for the recent market income levels and it can also tell you what you're capable of. Nevertheless, if the former standard stops you from accepting a new opportunity, you may cut yourself short. If you hadn't had that short-lived internship, for example, would you have been ecstatic with this new job offer?

Even if you'd held a job for many years, the new job is just that: an option among all other possibilities. The past is relevant and irrelevant at the same time. It's relevant because it's your guide for the general market for compensation for your skills. Yet, it's irrelevant because your past work isn't an option anymore, and if there were a better current offer, naturally, you'd take it.

Anchoring lets history influence decisions and the perception of happiness about your prospects. For example, if the price you expect to pay for a car is lower than what the new car costs, you'll be naturally disappointed. If you thought the car price was higher, you'd be thrilled despite the fact that the car price is the same in both scenarios.

New opportunities are distorted through the lenses not only of anchoring, but also **hindsight bias, belief perseverance, recency effect, conservativism, availability bias, house money effect**, and **loss aversion**. Bias effects your idea of happiness at work, and the amount of money you earn also impacts your happiness due to what you can afford. Spending money provides comfort and pleasure.

You will likely spend more time working than doing almost any other single activity in your life besides sleeping. Doing purposeful work can bring a natural sense of joy and fulfillment. Achievements – both work-related and otherwise – are an obvious source of happiness. Work can provide happiness just as much as it can interfere with it by soaking up a substantial part of your day doing something that you don't like. How much happiness you derive from work is up to you, based on whether you enjoy what you do or not.

Isn't job satisfaction a better indicator of happiness than the monetary compensation package, since it encompasses so much of our time? Obviously, the money and other benefits must meet your lifestyle needs. The amount you're paid must also be fair, if not competitive, in order to bring satisfaction, as well. If your colleague earns more money for the same work, you'll undoubtedly feel perturbed. The bottom line is that both money and fulfilling work are avenues to happiness. One can buy it and the other can create it intrinsically. Yet, both have the power to extinguish it.

As an investment practitioner, I've had the pleasure to work with a variety of individuals and families over the years. Many of them retire from work once they reach a certain savings level or when a pension plan matures. However, many others, who garner a sense of purpose and enjoyment in their careers, approach retirement planning from a different perspective. When work creates happiness directly, leaving it isn't as much of a motivation as when work simply provides income that can be traded for what makes you happy. Those who derive satisfaction from the work report that their goals are to work fewer hours or to be selective over the types of projects they engage with. It's still the same work, but on their terms.

This is particularly common among entrepreneurs and professionals who are recognized in their fields. They often see retirement as an option rather than a necessity.

These people approach retirement planning from the aspect of wanting to know how much they need to be financially secure. It's their baseline scenario. They want to have an eyeball on the date on which they could cash in their chips. The date is what provides the satisfaction of security. For these people, retirement planning is about achieving a comfortable lifestyle, hypothetically. Their work provides an essential aspect of happiness that they are in no hurry to relinquish.

Other individuals have a magic number that they want to achieve. Those are typically round numbers that their savings accounts are expected to reach. These goals are sometimes arbitrary, like saving a million dollars. More often, the retirement savings figure is based on a math equation accounting for expected returns, projected inflation, taxes, and the amount of savings needed to sustain a certain income level for the balance of their lives. The numbers provide support for their chosen lifestyle, and they usually end in a bunch of zeros.

The third group of savers measures themselves against their peers. Some clients inquire about their rank against their cohorts every time we meet. Interestingly, these particular clients notably ask for a comparison, while most others do not. These individuals want to know whether they are ahead of, or behind, the pack. Such benchmarks are more meaningful to them than a magic number. That is how they measure their success.

Regardless of how each of us arrives at the final goalpost, if you don't find happiness in your employment, retirement is a mathematical solution. If work produces income, and money produces happiness, then it follows that enjoyable work bestows happiness in two ways. When it doesn't, the best outcome is to save enough to end the unpleasant part as soon as possible.

Since 1987, when the minimum age to collect Canada Pension Plan (CPP) benefits dropped from 65 to 60, the average retirement age followed suit.[1] Not all of those individuals predicated their earlier retirement plans on the modest amount of CPP benefits they'd receive. If we've learned anything about anchoring, the mere endorsement of the earlier retirement age by government agents naturally impacts people's decision to take them up on it. *Sixty years old* stuck in people's minds as they grew toward it. It might as well have been a recommendation.

The trend to retire early goes beyond the availability of CPP benefits. During the 1990s, almost 10% more retirees left the workforce before reaching age 60 in the last half of the century than in the first. Without the financial resources, the decision to retire early is not possible without sacrifices. In this respect, it can also be said that you can buy happiness when you have enough money to afford to retire on the date of your choice.

Happiness during your working years is one thing, but living comfortably once the incoming money stops growing is another. Running out of money is the most significant risk that retirees face. Not surprisingly, the rising rates of divorce exacerbate these concerns. Imagine the impact of saving with a spouse over years or decades only to cut your accumulated wealth in half. Instead of running a single house with two people, that piggy bank is responsible for supporting the costs of two separate households.

Divorce isn't the only culprit. Longevity, low income, over-spending, lack of saving, and taking unnecessary risks add to the danger. Natural biases result in decisions to sell winning investments, adopt reasons to hold low-returning cash investments due to fear, or take unnecessary risks if you are facing a loss to try to make up ground. You can sometimes act like your own worst enemy.

Although biases cause financial losses over our lifetimes, **money illusion** may be the single highest impact judgment error when planning for your final years. Due to improvements in health care and a rising standard of living, North Americans enjoy healthier and longer lives. That means that the number of years that you spend in retirement are many more than earlier generations enjoyed.

Over time, the impact of inflation on the value of a dollar increases exponentially. It cuts into a retirement nest-egg, sometimes so deep that reducing spending doesn't stop the bleeding. Your tendency to view money in nominal terms – a dollar is worth a dollar – makes it difficult to appreciate how much inflation affects prices over long time frames. Money illusion is why you are at risk to underestimate how much savings you need for retirement.

The prospects of living out your final days with little control over your life limits the opportunities to find happiness. This isn't just because you cannot afford luxuries and lovely experiences to enhance your pleasure. Limited financial resources induce stress and anxiety that, in turn, affects your health and physical well-being. In the United States, eligibility age for Social Security depends on year of birth, gradually increasing from 65 to 67 if born in 1960 or later. US citizens are eligible for Medicare at 65, with varying costs (starting at free) based on level of insurance desired. In Canada, the social systems provide access to primary health care and other resources, for all citizens of every level of wealth. Despite the benefits of federal social assistance, free public health care, and provincially subsidized senior care homes, relying on government programs constrains your autonomy to make decisions and access privately offered health-related solutions.

For example, in-house nursing can allow people to remain in their homes longer, if they wish. Leaving a home environment prematurely can be destructive to your overall happiness and well-being. In the extreme examples, running out of money hits hardest by limiting choices, or rendering them to none.

Working with clients who have unplanned – or, in some cases, planned – financial collapse is like working with a patient diagnosed with a disease. Sometimes assets can be restored. In others, we manage to make it last as long as is reasonably possible. When a client insists on regular withdraws that will mathematically deplete their stockpile long before their life expectancy, there arises a natural conflict of interest. Nevertheless, people in such dire situations can often benefit from good advice.

In Ann's case, she had lived her life in a traditional, loving marriage during an era when working was uncommon for women. The Beatles rock band had just formed, but birth control was yet to be introduced. She was unaware of their financial affairs until her husband died at age 67.

Ann's eyes glittered through her fair features, and her white-blonde curls bounced youthfully as she walked. You'd never guess that she was 77 years old. Her demeanor, even during stressful conversations, was frank and witty. Decades earlier, her husband had arranged a life insurance policy, in case he predeceased her. The plan had a significant initial value. However, it was not enough after accounting for the inflated cost of living: $100,000 doesn't last very long after 40 years have rolled by. Ann withdrew a small amount of extra money that supplemented her pension plan to help with her rent and other costs. The expenses that she called *extras* didn't seem very extra.

Math is the great equalizer. It's defined and precise. You can't change the numbers to make them more amenable to our biased views. Ann was going to run out of money in the not-too-distant-future. "I know," she explained candidly. "I plan to run out of money. And when I do, my daughters will have to look after me." She was healthy, and there were good reasons to believe that she would live well into her nineties, as long as she remained healthy. "I want to live this way right now, and when I run out of money, I'll be older and won't care as much about what I have to spend," she tried to convince me. **Cognitive dissonance** at work.

Financial security is a critical component of happiness. Money illusion can cause unanticipated shortfalls in financial security and make the opportunity to feel happiness more difficult if you don't account for it. Our biases can affect our happiness when they undermine our financial decisions, especially related to our employment and retirement income. In each of these cases, reducing the impact of biases can positively impact your financial security and lead you to more happiness during the years of employment, as well as retirement.

Happiness and Spending Money

On the Monday morning before the March 2019 spring break, I woke up lying in bed with the birdsong alarm chirping away at the usual 5:25 a.m. (the hours I keep are an occupational hazard). I reached across to the bedside table for my iPhone and reading glasses. There, every news channel splashed a pop-up describing the second crash over the last few days, in which a Boeing Max 8 had again been plucked out of the air.

My children and I had planned our last spring break all together before universities swept them away, sitting on a beach in Maui. It took a moment for my pre-coffee brain to open the Air Canada phone-app and confirm the type of plane we were scheduled to board the upcoming Friday. My heart sank when I read the small print on the screen.

At the office, the week was filled with anxiety, tossing around what to do about our plans, like thousands of others set to fly on the Max 8 Boeing jets. Worry flooded the moments between managing portfolios and client meetings like water between stones. I cobbled together the airline disaster news reports, along with haphazard scientific research, and comments from pilots I knew well enough to call. I tried to create an understanding of the safety reports of the 737 Max 8 jet, to decide whether to board the plane on Friday with the souls of the three most critical people in my life.

By Wednesday, hundreds of travelers were relieved to hear that Canada had finally joined other nations in grounding these jets. Whether to fly on the Max 8 was no longer my decision, but the relief was short-lived. Thursday morning, an alert popped up on my iPhone screen confirming the outright cancellation of our flight from Calgary to Maui. It was the 737 Max 8 leg of our trip.

Realizing that a stampede of other travelers would share this same predicament, I hastily jumped on the travel app. Rushing through the limited selection of flights still available, I booked a one-way Hawaiian Air flight for the four of us out of Seattle for a ridiculous amount of money. Expedia's policies allowed for cancellations within 24 hours. Air Canada could still sort things out and provide an alternative to the grounded route, I reasoned as an alternative. Ultimately, it didn't. And while we waited to find that out, Air Canada's phone lines were so jammed that callers couldn't even remain on hold to wait for an attendant to answer their call.

Instead of sitting in a row on hard chairs at the Calgary airport with intermittent intercom announcements, limited food options, and the pervasive odor of cleaning fluids, we reclined on a lanai 10 feet from the ocean, just south of Old Lahaina, surrounded by tropical fragrance.

Despite our original plans falling through and the confusion in the days before take-off, the only risks to canceling were financial. The Airbnb waterfront accommodation on Puamana Beach was nonrefundable, and the expenses were long-since paid. **Sunk-cost bias** indicates that when no refund is available, we are more likely to spend additional funds to complete the trip than to cancel, if the price isn't prohibitive. Even then, there are emotional sunk costs rooted in the expectations of the plans. Anything you spend time earning or nurturing can trigger the same expected results of sunk-cost bias.

I had insurance coverage for travel arrangements, but the policy ultimately didn't cover this narrowly defined peril, as it turned out. Regardless, last-minute replacement flights are costly. Forking out any amount outside of the budgeted expense isn't always an option. Without the funds to buy the extra last-minute flights, the sense of loss – not only for the price of the accommodations but also for the demise of our plans – would have taken hold. If it doesn't buy you happiness directly, money certainly provides the opportunity to increase the possibility of happiness. At least, in our case, we were closer to happiness after buying the extra flights to take advantage of our holiday plans.

If money is tradeable for almost anything, then surely you can trade it for happiness. That's obvious when you spend money on things that bring you joy. Nevertheless, you may be dubious about this universal application for good reasons. It isn't as straightforward as it appears. Recall the miserable lottery winners, and the happily broke minimalists.

Of course, money can be used to hire people to do things that you don't enjoy. Isn't the removal of unhappiness the same as buying happiness? Money can similarly be used to free up your time from mundane or difficult tasks. If you have an unfortunately long driveway and you dread shoveling snow, the cost to hire a company to clear it both alleviates the grief felt for each snowfall and provides time for other enjoyable activities.

Spending money on time-savers is a measurable life improvement. Having a pizza delivered instead of having to cook for a busy family is liberating and anxiety reducing. With one child late for soccer practice and the other heading off to ballet, everyone in the family enjoys the freedom from setting the table, preparing the meal, and cleaning up afterward. Instead, they can focus on their relationships and the activities that they enjoy.

Naturally, free time can be used to pursue hobbies and interests that provide joy. However, as many people discovered during the pandemic of 2020, having more free time doesn't automatically mean that you're happier. Sitting in a confined condominium staring at the same walls every day – despite loads of free time – brought many people to their wits' end. If you're restricted from using free time to pursue relationships and activities that you enjoy, additional free time doesn't help much. Similarly, relaxing is useful if you need or want to relax. It isn't beneficial if you are already relaxed enough.

The day I met Dr. Mark Holder happened to be one in which the North American stock markets dropped in a rash of speculation. Mark's austere attire was in stark contrast to his infectious enthusiasm for life. He introduced himself as the most boring person alive, qualifying his claim with a mischievous grin, and, as all scientists do, with evidence. "Do you know anyone else who always responds with, *research indicates that. . .?*"

In a world obsessed with the causes of illness and grief, it is refreshing to meet someone undeterred by the positive – the optimistic – and focused on the study of happiness. A professor and worldwide leading expert on happiness, Mark is regularly called upon to speak at auspicious international engagements. Touted as the "Happiness Doctor" in articles and periodicals, his agent seemingly has no trouble procuring professional speaking engagements that thankfully feed his love of travel.

He doesn't drink or harbor the typical vices of the average Canadian, middle-aged man. He drives a Honda Civic because, as he puts it, "it's all I need." Juxtaposed to his conservative lifestyle, he confesses an unabashed passion for travel, exuberance for all types of life experiences, and a fierce generosity with friends. He exemplifies a life centered on his research findings about what makes people happy.

Dr. Holder's investigations suggest that money does indeed buy happiness, but it depends on how you spend it. He points first to an experiment in which participants were given money to spend. Those who were randomly selected to spend the funds on other people reported greater happiness than those who used it for themselves. These same researchers also found that spending more of your income on others predicted greater happiness in a Canadian national survey, as well as in separate studies that analyzed responses about spending after a windfall.[2]

He wasn't done yet. He then explained how money can also increase happiness when you spend it on experiences. Generally speaking, events, travel, and other encounters bring greater happiness than buying things. Again, he pointed out, it depends on the activity. Traveling to remote locations to dive in a shark-cage alongside prehistoric saltwater alligators might be the experience of a lifetime for some, while sending others to a state of terror. There's no happiness in fear.

If experiences categorically offer happiness, it is necessary that those experiences be meaningful to each of us individually. And when money brings you closer to those opportunities, then at least, money delivers a *pathway* to happiness.

In that same vein, opportunities to accomplish goals and to reach fulfillment or satisfaction naturally provide happiness. If you need money to execute one achievement or another, you could claim that money buys happiness in these cases as well.

Money can provide the opportunity for happiness, as you likely suspected. Nevertheless, as you also know from experience, money can just as easily create as many problems as it solves.

Happiness and Gluttony

Many people report that they could be happier if they just had a little more money. Presumably, that explains our willingness to spend millions of dollars on motivational speakers and financial gurus. Books proclaiming failproof strategies to buy real estate in the process of foreclosure fly off the shelves, making the authors wealthier from the book than from the strategy itself. Inspirational posters and ironic

T-shirts ask, "Why can't I be wealthy, instead of just good looking?" Get-rich-quick advice is an alluring path to the goals that we all seem to be chasing. Despite the fact that Americans are the wealthiest people in history, they are missing the lesson. Americans are categorically less happy than their level of wealth would otherwise dictate.[3]

Now that you understand more about how biases work, you probably realize that people don't always operate completely untethered when it comes to their spending habits. We are almost always affected by bias. Moreover, social pressures play a significant role in driving us to keep up with the Joneses. If you don't dress as well as the next applicant vying for your dream job, the notion of diminished success looms in the air. It may even cost you the advancement. Those who spend on luxury clothing or cars put others at a competitive disadvantage when impressions of the salesperson can close the sale. The decisions of a few wealthy people to buy these items push others to follow suit.

Technological developments for mass-produced goods have provided an incredible variety of products in unimaginable quantities compared to a hundred years ago. For example, it wasn't until the industrial revolution yielded an abundance of food that obesity became an epidemic. Similarly, the explosive production of products is directly responsible for the personal storage business becoming a multibillion-dollar industry across North America.

When retail shopping therapy brings little more than fleeting moments of delight, followed by days, months, or years of regret, beginning the moment your credit card payment is due, objects themselves may serve as reminders of what is already less valuable than it was on the day it was purchased. Changes in fashion, advancements in technology, and the realization that the item doesn't fit quite right renders your purchases to the discard pile. The importance of an inanimate object can never be more than you bestow on it. If the item continues to provide you with function or pleasure, you must continue to assign it a value. That may be more work than it's worth.

The sheer volume of goods that you can now access with the click of your computer mouse, automated payment system, and convenient home-delivery – enhanced by the **endowment effect** – has resulted in the accumulation of vast amounts of gear, objects, and other paraphernalia. Our cupboards and crawl spaces are stuffed with irresistible consumer purchases. This clutter fills our lives without satisfying the promise of joy that we had imagined. Some things in our lives provide pleasure and satisfaction, but much of it doesn't live up to the sales pitch that we used to convince ourselves to buy them.

If it isn't bad enough that we buy stuff we don't need, we are then reluctant to get rid of it. The popularity of shows depicting professionals hired to de-clutter people's homes and offices illustrates how difficult it is for us to part with our possessions. Perhaps our attachment to this clutter is at least partly due to loss aversion, sunk-cost bias, and the endowment effect. The pain of parting with belongings can even become a crippling, functional impairment when so many bits and bobbles litter our spaces that they are no longer livable. That, in turn, leads to personal distress. The *Diagnostic and Statistical Manual of Mental Disorders* (DSM-V) categorizes "hoarding as a compulsive spectrum disorder." However, it is easy to sympathize, in that hoarding is an extreme example of commonly occurring bias causing various degrees of distress.

A hundred years ago, there were no industrial buildings with square orange garage doors lining the side of the highway. The personal storage industry did not exist as it does today. Despite the steady increase in the size of residential homes, it wasn't until recently that people felt the need for off-site storage facilities.

Packing and stowing providers have a different point of view, however. The six Ds of storage demand are downsizing, death, divorce, displacement, disaster, and density. The fine people leasing storage units make us feel better about our overconsumption by blaming it on an *unanticipated personal micro-cycle*. It's easier to agree that it was beyond our control than to acknowledge that we simply bought too much stuff and refuse to part with it – reasoning to appease cognitive dissonance.

To compound matters, folks tend to hang onto unnecessary goods rather than disposing of them. The endowment effect makes valueless items worth saving. "I might need that in the future. I had better hang onto that so I don't have to rebuy it," we assure ourselves. Once we own stuff, we give it worth, even if the items are unnecessary. Thanks to the endowment effect, we tend to overvalue personal effects that we already own over the same article that we don't. Not only do we want to hang onto our extra goods, but we are also biased to overprice them when we try to get rid of them.[4]

In conventional negotiation tactics, sellers overstate and buyers understate the value at which they are willing to transact. Both parties aim to settle the negotiation at a favorable price. So, starting the bidding with a buffer to negotiate with is a darn good idea. It's also a good way to partly influence the negotiations due to anchoring.

The natural desire to avoid negative emotions causes us to behave in predictable and irrational ways – the sense of attachment to our belongings triggers loss aversion when we try to get rid of them. In turn, we come to value belongings above what the market would pay for them. The emotional bias of loss aversion is so pervasive that people weigh the damage of giving something up more heavily than the benefit of an equal gain.

Misplacing a $100 bill you could have sworn you zipped into the pocket of your jacket carries more significance than the joy of finding a $100 bill lying on the curb as you cross the street. The loss and the gain are numerically equal in value, but the loss packs a bigger punch. To equalize the emotional value between a gain and a loss, people typically need to win double the amount. That is to say, the pain we anticipate in loss is about twice as much as the joy of a gain.[5] This may be partly rooted in the mathematics of loss and gain. When you lose 20%, it takes 25% to return to where you started. In any event, losing money creates more unhappiness than gaining the same amount bestows.

You may know people who are always trying to give away unwanted items, saying, "Maybe you can use it." These people seemingly can't bear to throw out objects that still have usefulness, even though they don't want or need them anymore. Charities and stores that resell donations of used goods are an excellent way to recycle useful items and alleviate the emotional repercussions of our natural biases.

Since the Industrial Revolution, buying has become a frenzied experience. Those of us who have decided not to store unwanted purchases cart these things off to the landfill. The comedian Jerry Seinfeld describes our homes as nothing more than garbage-processing centers. "You buy new things. You bring them into your house, and you slowly Trashify them over time." Comedy often reflects our shared shortcomings:

> You repeat some of the lines the salesman used on you. But they don't sound the same when you say them. And you start to realize that maybe you're not going to be quite as keen on drying out fruit . . . as you thought you were going to be. It's

demoted to the closet. That's why we have [a closet]. So, we don't have to see all of the huge mistakes we have made. It starts on the shelf, where it's easy to get to. Then to the floor, where you start to step on it to reach things. You're now only interested in some other, newer item that is just beginning on its Journey to Junk.[6]

When you receive a gift, it's easier to pass along to a new recipient when you leave it in the original packaging. The term *regifting* was popularized in a 1995 *Seinfeld* episode about a label maker. The protagonist hastily rips open a thank-you gift from Tim Whatley for Superbowl tickets. His friend, Elaine, chimes in to agree that the label maker makes a great gift and that she had just given one to Tim Whatley last Christmas. Almost before she finishes her sentence, she realizes that Tim was passing along the present she had given him. He didn't like the gift enough to use it himself. The crafty description has been part of our vernacular ever since.

If money can buy happiness, it isn't the stuff we buy that provides it. How we imagine the things enhancing our lives is far more important in our quest. Consider the story you tell yourself when you're about to make a purchase. We convince ourselves of how it will enhance our life. It's sobering to remember that very same object will later lead to an unpleasant string of emotions as you manage its maintenance, storage, and ultimate disposal. Arguably, the stuff we buy can make us equally as unhappy as any level of joy it brought in the first place.

Health, Happiness, and Your Money

The availability of choice is hallmark for a developed nation. It's a meaningful benefit to be able to walk into your local grocer and select fresh cauliflower, kale, mushrooms, and four kinds of tomatoes in the dead of winter. The accessibility of plentiful nutritional goods – as well as a diversity of medical products and services – has notably improved our collective health well beyond last season's stored potatoes and root vegetables. Our improved standard of living enhances our general health and happiness overall.

It is common knowledge that lower stress and increased contentment affords a healthier and happier life. The most significant contributors to anxiety and stress are fear, misplaced exuberance, and regret. These emotions are also important motivations behind many of the behavioral biases that undermine financial decisions. **Loss aversion, possibility effect, certainty effect, overconfidence, hindsight bias, wishful thinking**, and **herd mentality** distract you from the goals that you listed in your **personal economic values (PEVs)**. Ultimately, your financial objectives and security are at stake. Biases such as loss aversion and hindsight bias can directly affect your happiness by generating angst and other negative emotions. The fear that comes with high debt levels relative to income, or the pit in your stomach when you face a financial loss, create an unpleasant distraction from your overall well-being.

Fear and worry not only reduce your quality of life, but can also shorten your expected lifespan. Stress, anxiety, depression, and negative thought patterns produce higher levels of cortisol.[7] When cortisol remains in your system over long periods, it begins to wreak havoc on everything from your immune system response to explosive interactions in personal relationships. Without happiness, your body begins to break down.

Genetics doesn't predestine the aging process any more than smoking guarantees premature death or fitness assures longevity. However, Dr. Elizabeth Blackburn's research on telomeres, for example, provides compelling hope and a clear motivation to reduce stress and increase happiness.

Dr. Blackburn began her most important work in pond scum, of all things. Beginning with sequencing the ends of DNA in microorganisms in the 1980s, she discovered that each chromosome terminates with a protective series that accelerates or decelerates the aging process. Her research applications today may be the most influential in promoting the impact of happiness on longevity. The telomeres are indicative of your health and well-being, but they also protect DNA during cell division.

During aging and stress, telomeres shorten and ultimately disappear, leaving you prone to physical deterioration and illness. Dr. Blackburn and Dr. Epel show that changes in your lifestyle can slow and even reverse the wear and tear on chromosome ends. Their extensive research shows that the common ways that we know to improve health also contribute to longer telomeres. Those include moderate exercise, eating well, and good sleeping routines. Beyond this motherly advice, they found conclusive evidence that positive mental habits effectively treat anxiety and depression. Those include focus and conscientiousness. They also indicate that cognitive psychological therapies, such as mindfulness practices, have a similar benefit. Eliminating the roots of stress can slow and reverse the effects that negative thought processes have on shortening these protective endings to your body's molecular structures.

According to a survey released in January 2019, Canadians are generally happy. High assessments of general happiness and financial security lead to a higher level of intimacy in personal relationships.[8] Sex and intimacy are not the only benefits of happiness. An increase in happiness results in improvements in your immune functioning, social relationships, sleep, cognitive flexibility, longevity, tolerance, creativity, and career advancements – a list so broad that some of the benefits enhance others in a self-augmenting cycle. Seniors who describe their health as very good or excellent, for example, also report higher levels of life satisfaction defined by their standard of living, life achievements, personal relationships, and health.[9]

Financial security creates happiness by reducing worry and emotional stress. It also provides the resources to improve health, increases access to joyful experiences, and increases health care options. Happiness, in turn, enhances personal relationships and our physical and mental well-being. Better health and wellness improve our standard of living, achievements, and life satisfaction.

So, you may not be surprised by the conclusion that financial security creates happiness.

How Much Is Enough?

"Show me your best diamonds. Money is no object."

Anonymous Billionaire

It appears that having excess cash is a carefree way to live. It looks like fun to overspend on luxury items without a blink of an eye. People are motivated to chase the spoils of superfluous living because the more money you have, the fewer restrictions you are seemingly tied to. Besides, it's fun to imagine a life where spending can be frivolous and blithe. If money can buy happiness, doesn't extra money buy more happiness?

There is no question that many people have fallen into believing that more trappings equal increased happiness. Yachts are twice as long as they were a few decades ago. Houses are larger, and we have more bathrooms. If you're middle-aged, you'll remember that an en suite bathroom was a relatively new development for average middle-class homes.

Yet, the question remains: Are we happier with more bathrooms? With longer boats?

Studies have shown that at a certain level of income, higher salaries don't increase happiness materially. Not surprisingly, at the point at which you can comfortably maintain your standard of living, increased happiness tapers off relative to each additional dollar earned. Once you cover the basic comforts, more income doesn't produce much more pleasure.[10]

As a society, excessive spending on luxury items means fewer resources are available for other purposes and other people. Aggregately, that detracts from everyone's happiness to a certain extent by creating unnecessary pollution and wasting natural resources, and fewer people enjoying the spoils.

Families with profound wealth ironically face the critical issue of thwarting the lifetime motivation of their children. They are worried about ruining their children's ambitions. Falling into extreme levels of wealth, especially at a young age, can undermine someone's purpose in life. The question of how much to bequeath is critical for families with wealth, when a gift that is disproportionate to the recipient's needs to be happy can have detrimental effects on their lives. Estate planning for those people almost always includes strategies to protect the ambitions and ultimate happiness for the next generation.

The other issue facing ultra-wealthy people is their role in social responsibility. When your money continues to compound, you can't help but to become richer. You can't spend it all. However, the behavioral tendencies that we outlined in the first three chapters plague everyone, regardless of wealth. It isn't as easy as it sounds to give millions of dollars away. Loss aversion still plays an insidious role. The same issues that affect each of us are not profoundly different as wealth increases.

Interestingly, having less money doesn't make you necessarily unhappier, either, as long as you have *enough*. But how much is enough when the bar keeps moving? The more money you have, the more you seem to need. As wealth rises, the target for enough money moves further away. When is enough *enough*?

Perhaps it is the way we are addressing the issues that is the root of the problem. Money is just money. It doesn't mean anything except what it can be exchanged for. The things that someone finds valuable, meaningful, or joyful may require money, but it doesn't necessarily require it.

When you have too little money, the obvious problems are well documented. Then, financial security can be defined as sustaining your basic needs and comforts. If we can combine this definition with the goals and objectives that you set out in the Eight Steps in Chapter 4, you will likely have a good idea of how much is *enough* for you.

What does financial security look like to you? A good starting point is to review your PEVs. Keep your beliefs about money in mind from Step Four of Chapter 4.

Your basic needs set the initial bar. That figure can be determined by making a list of your ongoing expenses and financial obligations. Add together your budget, financial obligations, and the costs for common comforts. How much money will it take to sustain these expenses?

Then consider the lifetime adventures, experiences, and acquisitions that are important for you to achieve in Step Two. Many of the things you want to achieve come with costs. Traveling the world, obtaining a degree, or starting a business each require a financial commitment. Add the amounts that you need to achieve each of those objectives, and when you'll need the money. Combine these values with the amount you need to maintain your financial security. And lastly, add a 10% buffer for unexpected health concerns and economic variability. This will total the amount of money that is *enough* money for you.

Wealth is inextricably tied to happiness for the simple reason that money can be traded for anything that provides your personal definition of happiness. It alleviates the issues of meeting basic survival needs. You can use it to create more opportunities to achieve experiences that bring joy. It can improve the outlook on your health or simply provide more options for all aspects of your well-being.

Money can buy happiness if you know how to spend it. However, you have to understand what makes you happy first. If you can raise more money while you discover what is joyful to you, all the better. All roads lead to Rome.

Interestingly, having just enough money seems to be better than having too much or too little. And, without the benefit of the calculation above, you may not discover how much is *enough* until after you've reached it. In any event, there is always math involved in determining how much money is enough for your financial security and to reach your key objectives, so it's helpful to find someone with a computer, a calculator, and some insights on financial planning. All the better if it is someone who understands the implications of behavior, finance, and your personal economic values.

It's also notable that your natural bias may disguise the happiness that is right under your nose. Hindsight bias often creates regret for no reason – the event was not preventable. Anchoring can prevent you from taking a new job or keeping one that you love because of the wages, even if they are fair. Comparisons to others compel you to buy stuff that you don't really want or need. Certainty effect makes it unbearable not to settle for a price much less than you could be awarded if you were able to withstand the tension and wait it out. And, loss aversion forces you to become risk-seeking, when cutting your losses would more closely align with your risk tolerance and your long-term objectives. Left unchecked, we are burdened with biased processes that produce unsavory results, despite our best intentions. If you can avoid these influences, you can enjoy more happiness, and reduce negative financial repercussions. This will help you retain more of your money and reduce financial stress in the process.

In the pages of this book, you have not only discovered some of the natural tendencies that affect your choices but also gained insights into how you can adopt simple yet strategic habits to limit their effects. Nevertheless, the best way to reduce biased decision-making is to limit the number of transactional choices you face over your lifetime.

By aligning your major decisions with your personal economic values, you are selecting the path toward your critical goals. In the process, you'll reduce the effects of biases along the way. You'll also find that this process will mitigate your risk and reduce your stress by limiting the number of transactional decisions that you confront.

Understand your personal economic values and stick to them, undistracted by your natural inclinations to take the path of least resistance. This is your opportunity to behave more consistently – like electricity – and create the best chance for lifelong happiness and financial success.

Notes

Chapter 1

1. D. Kahneman, *Thinking, Fast and Slow* (Anchor Canada, a division of Random House of Canada Limited, 2013).
2. Kahneman, *Thinking, Fast and Slow*.
3. R. Thaler, *Advances in Behavioral Finance Vol. II.* (Princeton: Princeton University Press, 2005).
4. D. Chambers and E. Dimson, *Financial Market History, Reflections on the Past for Investors Today* (CFA Institute Research Foundation, 2017).
5. A. Tversky and D. Kahneman, Judgment under uncertainty: Heuristics and biases. *Science* 185 (4157) (1974, September 27): 1124–1131.
6. Individual income tax return statistics for the 2020 tax-filing season. (2020). Retrieved from Government of Canada: https://www.canada.ca/en/revenue-agency/corporate/about-canada-revenue-agency-cra/individual-income-tax-return-statistics.html.
7. G. Hatala, *Made in Jersey: S&H Green Stamps – in the sixties, Americans were stuck on them*. (2013, November 4). Retrieved from New Jersey: https://www.nj.com/business/2013/11/made_in_jersey_sh_green_stamps.html.
8. D. Kahneman, J. L. Knetsch, and R. H. Thaler, Experimental test of the endowment effect and the Coase theorem. *The Journal of Political Economy* 98 (6) (1990, December): 1325–1348.

9. A. Draus, Canadian Tire money celebrates 60 years, *Global News* (2020, December 19), https://globalnews.ca/news/4409467/canadia-tire-money-60-years/.

Chapter 2

1. D. Kahneman, *Thinking, Fast and Slow* (Anchor Canada, a division of Random House of Canada Limited, 2013).
2. R. Falk and C. Konold, Making sense of randomness: Implicit encoding as a basis for judgment, *Psychological Review* 104 (2) (1997): 301–318.
3. R. Thaler and E. Johnson, Gambling with the house money and trying to break even: The effects of prior outcomes on risky choice, *Management Science* 36 (6) (1990, June): 643–660.
4. T. Odean, Are investors reluctant to realize their losses? *The Journal of Finance* 53 (5) (1998, October): 1775–1798.
5. H. Shefrin and M. Statman, The Disposition to sell winners too early and ride losers too long: theory and evidence, *The Journal of Finance* 40 (3) (1985, July): 777–790.
6. *Capital Gains – 2019 – Canada*, Government of Canada (2020, January 21), https://www.canada.ca/en/revenue-agency/services/forms-publications/publications/t4037/capital-gains.html#P279_29831.
7. Kahneman, *Thinking, Fast and Slow*.

Chapter 3

1. R. Beuhler, D. Griffin, and M. Ross, Exploring the planning fallacy: Why people underestimate their task completion times. *Journal of Personality and Social Psychology* (1994): 366–381.
2. N. D. Weinstein, Unrealistic optimism about future life events. *Journal of Personality and Social Psychology* 39 (5) (1980): 806–820.
3. *MLS®Home Price Index*. (2020, December 20). Retrieved from The Canadian Real Estate Association: https://www.crea.ca/housing-market-stats/mls-home-price-index/.
4. K. Case and R. Shiller, Is there a bubble in the housing market? *Cowles Foundation for Research in Economics Yale University* (2004): 299–362.
5. D. Chambers and E. Dimson, *Financial Market History, Reflections on the Past for Investors Today* (CFA Institute Research Foundation, 2017).
6. KOA, The 2017 North American Camping Report (2017). KOAPress Room.com.
7. Our Roots, Mountain Equipment Co-Op (2020, December 19). https://www.mec.ca/en/explore/our-roots.
8. P. Barnum, *The Life of P.T. Barnum, Written by Himself* (University of Illinois Press, 2000).

9. Barnum, *The Life of P.T. Barnum*.
10. B. Barber, T. Odean, and N. Zhu, *Systematic Noise*. Research Paper (University of California, Graduate School of Management/Haas School of Business, Berkeley/Davis, 2003).
11. C.W. and A.J.K.D, Economic history: Was tulipmania irrational? *The Economist* (2013, October 4), https://www.economist.com/free-exchange/2013/10/04/was-tulipmania-irrational.

Chapter 4

No notes

Chapter 5

1. R. Thaler and C. Sunstein, *Nudge* (Yale University Press, 2008).
2. Thaler and Sunstein, *Nudge*.
3. D. Chambers and E. Dimson, *Financial Market History, Reflections on the Past for Investors Today* (CFA Institute Research Foundation, 2017).
4. P. Stevens, When you sell during a panic you may miss the market's best days, CNBC (2020, March 7), https://www.cnbc.com/2020/03/07/when-you-sell-during-a-panic-you-may-miss-the-markets-best-days.html.
5. S. Benartzi and R. Thaler, Myopic loss aversion and the equity premium puzzle. In R. H. Thaler, *Advances in Behavioural Finance*, vol. II (New York: Princeton University Press, 2005), 203–221
6. Benartzi and Thaler, Myopic loss aversion and the equity premium puzzle, 203–221.
7. A. Thomas and P. Millar, Reducing the framing effect in older and younger adults by encouraging analytic processing, *The Journal of Gerontology Series B Psychological Sciences and Social Sciences* 67 (2) (2011, September): 139–149.
8. The Editors at Encyclopaedia Britannica. (n.d.). Apgar score system. Retrieved December 2020, from Encyclopaedia Britannica: https://www.britannica.com/science/Apgar-Score-System.
9. M. AlKhars, N. Evangelopoulos, R. Pavur, and S. Kulkarni, Cognitive biases resulting from the representativeness heuristic in operations management: an experimental investigation, *Psychology Research and Behavior Management* 12 (2019, April 10): 263–276.

Chapter 6

1. K. Cremers, J. Fulkerson, and T. Riley, CFA, Challenging the conventional wisdom on active management, *Financial Analyst Journal* 75 (4) (2019, July 18).

2. B. Liu, Can top-performing funds stay on top over time? *S&P Global* (2020, July 1). https://www.spglobal.com/en/research-insights/articles/can-top-performing-funds-stay-on-top-over-time.
3. S&P Dow Jones Indices, S&P Global (2020, December), from: https://www.spglobal.com/spdji/en/indices/equity/sp-500/#overview.
4. M. Gladwell, Complexity and the ten-thousand-hour rule, *The New Yorker* (2013).
5. D. Kahneman, *Thinking, Fast and Slow* (Anchor Canada, a division of Random House of Canada Limited, 2013).
6. J. Arlen and S. Tontrup, Does the endowment effect justify legal intervention? The debiasing effect of institutions, *The Journal of Legal Studies* 44 (1) (2015): 143–182.

Chapter 7

1. *Perspectives on Labour and Income – Fact-sheet on retirement.* (2000). Retrieved December 2020, from Statistics Canada: https://www150.statcan.gc.ca/n1/pub/75-001-x/00502/4235045-eng.pdf.
2. E. Dunn, L. Arknin, and M. Norton, Spending money on others promotes happiness, *Science* 319 (5870) (2008, March 21): 1687–1688.
3. R. H. Frank, *Luxury Fever: Why Money Fails to Satisfy in an Era of Excess* (New York: Free Press, 1999).
4. D. Kahneman, *Thinking, Fast and Slow* (Anchor Canada, a division of Random House of Canada Limited, 2013).
5. Kahneman, *Thinking, Fast and Slow.*
6. Jerry Seinfeld, *Is this Anything?* (New York, London, Toronto, Sydney, New Delhi: Simon and Schuster, 2021).
7. E. Blackburn and E. Epel, *The Telomere Effect: A Revolutionary Approach to Living Younger, Healthier, Longer* (Grand Central Publishing, 2018).
8. T. G. Group, Survey of Canadians' happiness, *The Globe and Mail* (2018, July), https://www.theglobeandmail.com/files/contentstudio/editorial/goodnews/happiness-survey/Globe-and-Mail_Happiness-Survey_July-12-2018-oct24.pdf
9. Government of Canada, *Health Fact Sheets Life Satisfaction, 2016.* Life Satisfaction, 2016 (2017, September 27), https://www150.statcan.gc.ca/n1/pub/82-625-x/2017001/article/54862-eng.htm
10. Jebb, L. Tay, E. Diener, and S. Oishi, Happiness, income satiation and turning points around the world. *Nature Human Behaviour 2* (2018, January): 33–38. Retrieved from Nature: https://www.nature.com/articles/s41562-017-0277-0

Index